D1165412

American Sign Language and Early Literacy

American Sign Language and Early Literacy

A Model Parent-Child Program

Kristin Snoddon

Gallaudet University Press
Washington, D.C.

Gallaudet University Press
Washington, DC 20002
http://gupress.gallaudet.edu

Library of Congress Cataloging-in-Publication Data

Snoddon, Kristin.
  American Sign Language and early literacy : a model parent-child program
/ Kristin Snoddon.
     p. cm.
  Includes bibliographical references and index.
  ISBN 978-1-56368-527-9 (hbk. : alk. paper)—ISBN 1-56368-527-2 (hbk. : alk.
paper)—ISBN 978-1-56368-528-6 (e-book)—ISBN 1-56368-528-0 (e-book)
     1. American Sign Language.   2. Sign language acquisition.   3. Early
childhood special education.   4. Special education—Parent participation.
5. Deaf children—Language.   6. Children of deaf parents—Language.
I. Title.

    HV2476.4.S66   2012
    371.91'246—dc23   2011048173

Chapter 2 originally appeared as "American Sign Language and Early Intervention" in *The Canadian Modern Language Review* (64[4], 581–604).

∞ The paper used in this publication meets the minimum requirements of
American National Standard for Information Sciences—Permanence of Paper
for Printed Library Materials, ANSI Z39.48-1984.

It is only when the oppressed find the oppressor out and become involved in the organized struggle for their liberation that they begin to believe in themselves. This discovery cannot be purely intellectual but must involve action; nor can it be limited to mere activism, but must include serious reflection: only then will it be a praxis.

—Paolo Freire

Contents

Acknowledgments

My INVOLVEMENT with the field of ASL and early literacy is due largely to the support and inspiration provided by Joanne Cripps and Anita Small. The staff and board members of the Ontario Association of the Deaf have also provided me with myriad forms of support. I wish to convey special thanks to Jennifer Jackson for having hired me in the summer of 2006 to write a discussion paper about Ontario public service gaps to young Deaf children that became a foundation for my study. I am also indebted to Jim Cummins and to Eunice Jang for the guidance they provided for my research.

I could not have conducted my study without the collaboration of the Ontario Cultural Society of the Deaf or of the parents who participated with their children in our ASL Parent-Child Mother Goose Program. Kevin Canning volunteered his time and expertise to film our program, while Jason Theriault provided invaluable technological assistance throughout and beyond my study.

Finally, I would like to thank my husband, Christopher Pellow, who was there for me in the beginning and saw me through to the end of my study. With his love and support my endeavors seem more possible and worthwhile.

Introduction

1

THIS BOOK IS about an American Sign Language (ASL) literacy program for Deaf and hearing parents and young children in Ontario, Canada. Underlying this subject are several different lines of inquiry. First, this book describes the present-day context of infant hearing screening and early intervention services for Deaf children and their parents, and the impact these public services have for participants in the program. Second, the processes and outcomes of the ASL Parent-Child Mother Goose Program are described in terms of a counterdiscourse to the dominant discourse of early intervention policy for Deaf children and their parents. This counterdiscourse includes the distinct roles taken by Deaf and hearing parents during the program and by the program leader as a Deaf adult and ASL instructor working to facilitate emergent ASL literacy.

In using the capital *D* for every instance of the word *Deaf*, instead of only when discussing individuals who are members of the signing Deaf community, this book follows the convention established by Joanne Cripps (2000). I similarly use the capital *D* not to place a particular identity on particular individuals, but rather to indicate that signed language and Deaf culture are the birthright of every Deaf person by virtue of him or her having been born Deaf or having become Deaf in childhood, whether or not he or she has been exposed to Deaf culture.

My interest in early ASL literacy is based in part on my professional experience with a Deaf community organization (referred to throughout the book as DCO) that in 2003 founded the ASL Parent-Child Mother Goose Program for teaching ASL rhymes and stories to parents and young children. From 2001–2005, I was employed by DCO as a program coordinator. In this position, I was responsible for organizing training workshops for ASL instructors who worked with families under the Ontario government's Infant Hearing Program. I also coordinated the program. This program builds on the contributions of Deaf linguist and poet Clayton Valli, whose seminal work in ASL poetry identified ASL rhyme and meter. The program was also developed in collaboration with the original, spoken-language Parent-Child Mother Goose Program and follows the original program's principles and main objectives. In the Parent-Child Mother Goose Program, groups of parents and caregivers are taught oral rhymes, songs, and stories in order to promote parent–child bonding and positive communication, and support children's language development. The ASL Parent-Child Mother Goose Program focuses on language interaction between parents and young children using ASL rhymes and stories and aims at developing a literary level of ASL while supporting the bond between parent and child.

When DCO's program funding was cut in 2005, I was filled by a sense of injustice at the uneven allocation of public resources for ASL programs and services for families with Deaf children. This sense of injustice is partly why I adopted an ethnographic action research approach for my study. Action research is practical; it aims at producing solutions to real problems. Additionally, action research involves participants as active subjects. Most research in Deaf education consists of quantitative studies that emphasize Deaf people's perceived deficiencies. A qualitative, collaborative approach stands in contrast to this body of research. Moreover, ethnography is one of the most effective means of studying language practices and language communities (Heath, 1983).

This book therefore tells the story of parents and children participating in an early ASL literacy program in the fall of 2007. This participant group consisted of two families with Deaf parents and Deaf children, one Deaf parent with a hearing child, and three hearing parents with Deaf or hard of hearing children who were registered with a Deaf service agency in the province of Ontario. The program leader, a Deaf adult and ASL instructor, was also a participant, along with me as a researcher. This book also describes an action research methodology that might be used by other individuals seeking to effect change in their communities. This methodology may be termed *openly ideological research* (Lather, 1986), but this is not to say that other forms of research, including the above-mentioned quantitative studies, are any less ideological. It is simply that I seek to be clear with my intentions: along with other participating individuals in the program, to forward an emancipative literacy for Deaf children, their families, and their community. This book shows how ASL literacy can function as such an emancipative literacy.

ASL Literacy

It is important to discuss how, for this book's purposes, the term *literacy* is defined in relation to ASL. Any view of literacy is inherently political (Gee, 2008). Reserving the term *literacy* for languages involving reading and writing often goes hand in hand with unsubstantiated claims that print literacy alone leads to, among other so-called higher-order thinking skills, logical and rational thinking and the abstract use of language. Such a definition for literacy can uphold as well as mask relations of power that reproduce and maintain systemic inequities, because literacy pedagogy has often been restricted to formalized, monolingual forms of language (New London Group, 1996), which all students do not access on an equal basis.

This definition also masks how literacy is a socially constructed and socially situated process: It is not reasonable to locate literacy at the level of individual or psychological abilities, or to view literacy as something that can be assessed in terms of how much someone has of it. Rather, literacy practices are integrated with and constitute part of wider practices that involve forms of communication and interaction, and values and beliefs (Gee, 2008).

With respect to the need for a broad, sociocultural understanding of ASL literacy, it is equally true that ASL texts and the various ways of reading them are the collective social and historical invention of Deaf, ASL-using people. As in the general case of literacy practices, Deaf learners of ASL learn to interpret texts in ways that reflect the reading conventions of the Deaf community and its social settings. ASL literacy is therefore a social practice that must be acquired through social and cultural participation.

Conceptions of ASL literacy are tied but not limited to the recognition of ASL as a language. Research in signed language linguistics has validated signed languages as full languages and in part has served as a justification for their use as languages of instruction for Deaf students. Starting in the 1990s, ASL and English bilingual education programs have been provided in several Canadian provinces and U.S. states. In Ontario, since 1998, the ASL Curriculum Team serving the provincial schools for Deaf students has focused on creating a language arts curriculum in which ASL linguistic structure is studied in addition to ASL literature, ASL texts, and ASL media arts and technology (Small & Mason, 2008). The ASL Curriculum posits a view of ASL pedagogy that aligns with Jim Cummins's (2001) definition of academic language learning: supporting the comprehension of linguistically and conceptually demanding texts and the ability to use the language in an accurate and coherent way. This view of ASL as an academic language stands in contrast to the position that ASL is only a conversational language in which literacy is not possible.

ASL literacy can be defined in terms of functional, cultural, and critical literacy (Small & Cripps, 2004). From this perspective, *functional ASL literacy* may be viewed as ASL decoding and production skills, whereas *cultural literacy* may be defined as the ability to understand and appreciate the cultural significance of ASL literature (among other aspects of ASL culture). *Critical literacy* may be viewed as the ability to analyze, critique, and respond to the values inherent in ASL literature and other kinds of texts, from the perspective of an ASL user. In the Ontario ASL Curriculum, knowledge of language structure is distinguished from literacy, and ASL literacy is aligned with acquisition of the cultural value of ASL and other languages' literary works (Small & Mason, 2008). In other words, the ASL Curriculum's concept of ASL literacy takes a view of language learning that moves beyond functional literacy or language skills to encompass cultural as well as critical literacy. This view of literacy postulates an ASL discourse rather than simply (varying degrees of) knowledge of ASL. As James Gee (2008) defines them, "Discourses are ways of behaving, interacting, valuing, thinking, believing, speaking [and signing], and often reading and writing" that particular groups of people accept as instantiations of particular identities (p. 3).

How the ASL Parent-Child Mother Goose Program views language and literacy is also a central issue for this book. To a large extent, the focus of the program is not on teaching ASL but on teaching ASL poems and stories and some facets of the culture of Deaf ASL users—a focus that centers on cultural literacy. This focus on cultural rather than simply functional literacy or ASL skills is a key distinction for the many Deaf children of hearing parents for whom first-language acquisition and socialization are not the inevitable, taken-for-granted process that they largely are for hearing children acquiring spoken language or for Deaf children of Deaf parents. The program's focus became an issue for those participating parents who, like many other hearing parents of Deaf children, had no other resources or support for learning ASL.

For these parents and their children, the program blurred the distinction between what Gee (2008) terms primary and secondary discourses, where a *primary discourse* is acquired early in life within a "primary socializing unit" (p. 156). A primary discourse provides both our initial sense of identity and the basis of our particular culture's vernacular language with which we act out our particular culture's vernacular identity. *Secondary discourses* are acquired later in life, in a more public forum than a primary discourse's primary socializing unit. Secondary discourses are acquired within institutions, such as schools, that are part of wider communities. Gee defines literacy as mastery of a secondary discourse. Since there are many secondary discourses and all individuals possess a range of some (but not other) secondary discourses, literacy is always plural, and it involves a range of text and technologies including but not limited to print.

The young Deaf, hard of hearing, and hearing children who participated in the program's ASL literature activities and interacted with its community of Deaf and hearing ASL users were in the process of acquiring not only ASL but also an ASL discourse. For many of these child participants, the ASL discourse learned in our program can be viewed as primary as well as secondary because it was tied to their exposure to an accessible first language—a process of exposure in which their parents, Deaf and hearing, played a key role. In addition, Deaf adults from outside of the children's family unit who nonetheless shared a distinct kind of knowledge and experience with the Deaf child participants played a central role in transmitting this ASL discourse. Most Deaf children lack full access to social interaction until they encounter an ASL environment. In such an environment, Deaf children enjoy full communication and a change in status from outcast or deviant to participating members of a rich culture with its own heritage, shared meanings, experiences, and values (Lane, Hoffmeister, & Bahan, 1996). In other words, historically, Deaf children of hearing parents have often acquired an ASL discourse when they are away from the family unit of intimates and immersed in a residential school environment where they interact with Deaf adults and other Deaf students. This ASL discourse serves as the basis for secondary discourses, including academic ASL and English discourses.

This book describes a family ASL literacy program that seeks to engender an ASL discourse among young children and their parents who may not otherwise have access to early ASL literacy resources. This ASL discourse may be primary as well as secondary for the child participants in the program, but it is a secondary discourse for hearing parents learning ASL. For Deaf parent participants, the secondary, community-based ASL discourse presented by the program may in turn shape their own primary discourse that they pass on to their children. As I show in this book, the key aspect of this ASL discourse is how it came to function as a counterdiscourse to the dominant discourse of early intervention programming and policy for Deaf children

The next chapter discusses the overall context of infant hearing screening and early intervention programs and gaps in service to young Deaf children and their families. Chapter 3 presents the framework of discourses that work to pathologize ASL and Deaf bilingualism. Chapter 4 introduces the setting and participants in my participatory action research study. Chapter 5 presents themes that emerged regarding the issues of gatekeepers— individuals and institutions that restrict parents' and Deaf children's access to ASL—and public resources for supporting ASL literacy in Deaf children and their parents. Chapter 6 describes the theme of name signs and the Deaf cultural space that emerged in the course of the program as a counterdiscourse. Chapter 7 describes child response to the program and the roles taken by Deaf and hearing mothers and the program leader. Chapter 8 summarizes the implications of these findings in regard to the benefits of early ASL literacy programming for Deaf children and their families.

2

ASL and Early Intervention

IN HEARING CHILDREN, the development of English literacy is preceded by language skills including metalinguistic and phonological awareness, and by a broad first-language vocabulary and opportunities for verbal interaction (Snow, Burns, & Griffin, 1998). Developing minority-language children's first-language expertise is crucial to learning how to read in English. Because an impoverished first-language foundation is often the source of difficulties experienced by beginning Deaf readers, and a strong relationship between ASL proficiency and English literacy has been established in Deaf students, educational and intervention programs for young Deaf children should be designed to facilitate emergent literacy in both languages.

However, research on the development of signed language in Deaf children appears to be slowing in countries that are most quickly embracing cochlear implants for this population (Schick, Marschark, & Spencer, 2006). As researchers reach a general consensus regarding the advantages of Deaf children's learning a signed language early in childhood, public policy is not keeping pace with these developments. In particular, a number of issues have been identified related to the Ontario government's Infant Hearing Program (IHP) and its lack of explicit policy regarding the provision of ASL services to Deaf infants and young children who receive cochlear implants.

Established in May 2000, the IHP provides universal infant hearing screening and early intervention services to young children with hearing loss and their families (Hyde, 2002). As the first public initiative of this kind in Canada, the IHP is part of a larger network of universal infant hearing screening programs that were introduced in several countries at the beginning of the 21st century. Prior to the introduction of this technology, it was rare for an infant to be identified as Deaf in the first year of life (Meadow-Orlans, 2004). The significance of early identification of hearing loss and the provision of intervention services lies in their implications for the early education of Deaf children, of whom many are at risk for delays in language development regardless of the degree of their hearing loss (Spencer, 2004). There is nothing inherent in hearing loss that restricts language development. Delayed language development in Deaf children is often a result of their delayed exposure to a visual language that they can access and process effectively. Yet, as I will show in this chapter, the decision-making bodies that set policy for the early education of Deaf children are not guided by relevant research on Deaf children's language acquisition or bilingual development, and early intervention programs may not provide a well-informed or adequate range of options to parents and children.

The children I refer to in this chapter are mainly those with severe to profound levels of hearing loss, defined as encompassing the 70- to 90-decibel-and-above range (Goldin-Meadow & Mayberry, 2001). However, hard of hearing children—who are also featured here—span a wide range of audiological thresholds, from 30- to 90-decibel hearing losses (Blamey, 2003).

Background

Education for Deaf students in Canada and the United States has often followed a monolingual philosophy. Historically, this has meant failing to support the use of native signed languages of the Deaf community in classrooms or educational programs for Deaf students, due to widespread conceptions that learning a signed language will hinder the development of spoken and written language skills. However, Deaf children lack access to the auditory base that hearing children have for acquiring a spoken language.

Even young children with relatively mild degrees of hearing loss have been shown to be at risk for difficulties in language development due to limited access to language through the auditory channel (Bess, Dodd-Murphy, & Parker, 1998; Meadow-Orlans, Mertens, & Sass-Lehrer, 2003; Spencer, 2004). As a consequence, many young Deaf children fail to receive full and timely access to language in any modality.

In Ontario, infants and young children with cochlear implants have frequently not been able to receive public support for learning ASL. The rationale for this phenomenon is allegedly the stance taken by practitioners of auditory-verbal therapy (AVT) against Deaf children's learning of signed language. AVT is an intervention approach for children with hearing loss that emphasizes spoken language development through early identification, amplification, and intensive speech therapy. Fostering educational and social inclusion with hearing peers is one of the primary goals of this intervention approach (Eriks-Brophy, 2004).

Cochlear implant teams at Ontario children's hospitals have required Deaf children who undergo this surgery to enroll in AVT. Although an IHP senior program consultant has cited the refusal of AV therapists to treat children who are learning signed language (M. Stein, letter to the Ontario Association of the Deaf, August 23, 2006), the decision to not publicly fund ASL services for children with cochlear implants has appeared to be an operational, if not explicit IHP policy. ASL services are in fact available to other Ontario families with Deaf children, through part-time family ASL instructors under contract with the IHP.

Profile of Deaf Children

The majority of Deaf children are born to hearing parents with little or no knowledge of signed language and are not exposed to a fully accessible language until later in life. One study of severely to profoundly Deaf children in Ontario found that 93% of these children were initially enrolled in auditory-oral intervention programs and 67% of Deaf preschool children were educated orally; the figures dropped to 58% for elementary school children and 31% for high school students. Between the early preschool years and adolescence, 62% of Deaf children shifted from oral programs to programs with sign support or ASL (Akamatsu, Musselman, & Zweibel, 2000). From these statistics, it can be deduced that the majority of Deaf children begin school deprived of access to a full language and fall steadily behind their hearing peers as they progress through grade levels. As a consequence, these students are often transferred to a signed language environment for remedial instruction when valuable years for language learning have been lost. Although this study was conducted prior to the establishment of infant hearing screening and early intervention services in Ontario, to date there have been no follow-up studies published to suggest that the educational profile of most Deaf children has significantly changed.

Researchers have documented the effects of delayed first-language acquisition on Deaf people's language performance and processing skills (e.g., Mayberry, 1993; Mayberry & Eichen, 1991; Newport, 1990, 1991). In fact, research with Deaf individuals who acquired a signed language at different ages has been used to demonstrate the critical period hypothesis, which has been difficult to test in the case of hearing children who are normally exposed to a first language from birth. The *critical period hypothesis* postulates that the ability to fully acquire a language is limited to the period from infancy to puberty (Lenneberg, 1967). Other researchers have presented discussions of innate constraints on learning, using evidence from studies of ASL learners of different ages (Emmorey, 2002; Mayberry, 1994; Morford & Mayberry, 2000). In addition to offering support for a critical period for language learning, these studies indicate that the long-term effects of delayed first-language acquisition are much more detrimental than the effects of acquiring a second language late in childhood.

Lack of access to a signed language environment, rather than any inherent deficiencies in Deaf children's language learning or developmental abilities, is behind the problems faced by Deaf late first-language learners. Natural signed languages such as ASL and Langue des signes québécoise, or Quebec sign language (LSQ), demonstrate the same linguistic properties as spoken languages, including phonetic, phonemic, syllabic, morphological, syntactic, discourse, and pragmatic levels of organization (Newport & Meir, 1985; Petitto, 1994). Research with Deaf children who are exposed to signed languages from birth demonstrates that they acquire these languages on an identical maturational time course as hearing children acquiring spoken language (Morford & Mayberry, 2000; Newport & Meier, 1985; Petitto, 2000; Schick, 2003; Spencer, 2004; Volterra & Iverson, 1995). From birth to the age of 3 years and beyond, speaking and signing children exhibit identical stages of language acquisition, including the syllabic babbling stage from 7 to 11 months; the first word stage from 11 to 14 months; and the first-two-word stage from 16 to 22 months (Petitto, 2000).

These findings for the normal language development of infants exposed to signed language are supported by the well-documented superior performance of Deaf children of Deaf parents over Deaf children of hearing parents on tests of academic achievement, reading and writing, and social development (e.g., Kourbetis, 1982; Weisel, 1988). A review of the body of literature regarding Deaf children of Deaf and hearing parents shows higher English literacy abilities in native ASL users compared to Deaf children who learn ASL later in life (Israelite & Ewoldt, 1992). These findings across multiple studies showed consistently superior results for Deaf children of Deaf parents despite the lower socioeconomic status of these parents (Zweibel, 1987). Researchers observe the phenomenon of Deaf children of Deaf parents having superior English literacy abilities to Deaf children of hearing parents, interesting because English is not the first group's native language and most children of hearing parents receive more intensive auditory-oral training in English (Newport & Meier, 1985). However, more recent studies of highly ASL-fluent Deaf children of hearing parents suggest that a well-developed language foundation in ASL enables Deaf students to reach higher levels of English literacy regardless of parental hearing status (Singleton, Supalla, Litchfield, & Schley, 1998; Strong & Prinz, 1997, 2000).

While there has been some debate on whether young children exposed to signed language exhibit a linguistic advantage when compared to children exposed to only spoken language (Anderson, 2006), this notion is disputed by other researchers (Volterra & Iverson, 1995; Volterra, Iverson, & Castrataro, 2006). Rather, these writers argue, prelinguistic gestural communication is used by all children in the earliest stages of language development, and this has erroneously been taken for a signed language advantage. Language development in Deaf children exposed to signed language from birth is strikingly parallel to language development in hearing children exposed to spoken language. However, a 2-year longitudinal study of more than 130 families with hearing infants suggests that increased exposure to symbolic gesturing benefits infants' receptive and expressive spoken language development (Goodwyn, Acredolo, & Brown, 2000). Another argument states that although increased exposure to gestural input does not accelerate first-word production in either signed or spoken languages, it can facilitate vocabulary growth later in development (Abrahamsen, 2000). It is clear that enhanced experience with gestural communication does not interfere with, and may facilitate, spoken language development (Volterra et al., 2006). However, Deaf children exposed to gestural communication but not the systematic linguistic input provided by a natural signed language exhibit delays in their language development when compared to hearing children and to Deaf children exposed to signed language from birth (Volterra et al., 2006).

Bilingual Proficiency and Signed Language

Research demonstrating the consistent benefits of early signed language acquisition by Deaf children refutes the position that learning ASL hinders spoken or written English development. Studies show that learning signed language has a positive effect on young Deaf children's spoken language skills (Preisler, Tvingstedt, & Ahlström, 2002; Yoshinaga-Itano & Sedey, 2000). Preisler and colleagues (2002) studied patterns of communication for 22 preschool children who had received cochlear implants between ages 2 and 5 over a 2-year period. This study took place in Sweden, where parents must establish some signed language in communication with their child in order to be considered for a cochlear implant (Swedish National Board of Health & Welfare, 2000). The researchers observed that the children in their study who developed the most spoken language also had well-developed signed language skills. Although signed language by itself was not a guarantee for the development of spoken language, the children who had insufficient or discontinued signed language development also had very little or no spoken language abilities. It was also observed that when children with little signed language developed better signed language abilities, spoken language also increased.

Yoshinaga-Itano and Sedey (2000) investigated the relationship between speech development and various demographic and developmental factors, including mode of communication, in children aged 14 to 60 months. These researchers found that expressive signed and spoken language ability was a significant predictor of speech development in young Deaf and hard of hearing children. Earlier studies also show a significant relationship between linguistic ability—including verbal communicative intentions, mastery of the rules of syntax, and strong skills in vocabulary and semantics—and speech intelligibility in Deaf children (cited in Yoshinaga-Itano & Sedey). The available research is consistent with the position that access to a signed language increases overall linguistic ability in Deaf children, and it certainly increases vocabulary levels (Anderson, 2006; Watkins, Pittman, & Walden, 1998). A high level of linguistic competence is linked to speech perception abilities in Deaf and hard of hearing children with hearing aids and cochlear implants (Blamey, 2003). Studies comparing the speech perception abilities of deafened adults to those of Deaf and hard of hearing children show lower scores for children as compared to deafened adults, even when more residual hearing is present in the children (e.g. Blamey et al., 2001). An advanced knowledge of phonology, syntax, and semantics is needed in order for Deaf and hard of hearing children with hearing aids and cochlear implants to comprehend spoken language input.

The use of signed language has been shown to positively affect language development and social and emotional development for preschool hard of hearing children (Preisler & Ahlström, 1997). The children in this study were bilingual in spoken Swedish and Swedish sign language and exhibited flexibility in their use of two languages. These children's patterned and purposeful code-switching to match their communication partner's prerequisites and the communicative context is mirrored by other studies of young bilingual hearing children that show differential and appropriate use of their developing languages (e.g., Comeau, Genesee, & Lapaquette, 2003; Genesee, Nicoladis, & Paradis, 1995).

The Relationship Between ASL Proficiency and English Literacy

In addition to positively influencing spoken language development, proficiency in ASL has been empirically shown to support English literacy in Deaf students (Hoffmeister, 2000; Padden & Ramsey, 1998, 2000; Singleton et al., 1998; Strong & Prinz, 1997, 2000). This body of research, showing a positive correlation between high levels of ASL proficiency and English literacy skills, is supported by literature showing higher English literacy abilities in native ASL users compared to Deaf children who learn ASL later in life. This research is also supported by various studies dating from 1916 that measure Deaf students' reading and language skills (Chamberlain & Mayberry, 2000). A link between signed language and reading is evident even in these very early studies. The hypothesis that ASL functions like any other first language when brought to the task of learning a second language is supported by several researchers (e.g., Goldin-Meadow & Mayberry, 2001; Hoffmeister, 2000; Morford & Mayberry, 2000). This research also indicates that Cummins's (1981) *interdependence hypothesis,* which states that proficiency in a first language transfers to proficiency in a second language when there is adequate exposure to and motivation to learn the second language, applies in the case of ASL and English.

However, Mayer and Wells (1996) presented a theoretical argument against the applicability of the interdependence hypothesis in this regard. For these authors, the interdependence hypothesis assumes that a written version of the first language is present to support literacy in the second language, as it is usually not for ASL (although ASL glossing and signwriting systems have been devised, these have not been widely employed by educational programs for Deaf students). These writers also interpret the hypothesis as requiring access to the spoken form of the second language, which is lacking for a large proportion of Deaf students. Because of the "double discontinuity" (Mayer & Wells, p. 104) between ASL and English, these writers argue, the conditions assumed by the hypothesis cannot be met and ASL does not support learning of English.

These claims are not, however, empirically supported by the research studies mentioned above. Cummins (2005) explicitly states that his interdependence hypothesis does not refer simply to developing language skills such as decoding written text, but "a deeper conceptual and linguistic proficiency that is strongly related to the development of literacy in the majority language"

(p. 4). He lists five types of possible transfer from the first to the second language, depending on the sociolinguistic situation:

• Transfer of conceptual elements
• Transfer of metacognitive and metalinguistic strategies
• Transfer of pragmatic aspects of language use
• Transfer of specific linguistic elements
• Transfer of phonological awareness

Additionally, Cummins refers to his hypothesis in the context of dissimilar languages like English and Turkish, where "transfer will consist primarily of conceptual and cognitive elements (e.g., learning strategies)" (p. 5). But the matter of which additional types of transfer may apply in the case of ASL and English is an area that merits further study. For instance, fingerspelling and other ASL-based bridging techniques may encourage transfer of specific linguistic elements as well as provide a visual phono-logical bridge (Haptonstall-Nykaza & Schick, 2007; Padden & Ramsey, 1998, 2000). Deaf children's access to the phonology of a signed language may provide the linguistic and cognitive basis for successful use of a written second language (McQuarrie & Parrila, 2009).

Nonetheless, early intervention and pedagogical approaches for Deaf children have often assumed a *separate underlying pro-ficiency model* of bilingual development (Cummins, 2001). In this model, first- and second-language proficiencies are separate from each other, and learning of one language does not support learn-ing of the other. As an example of this view, one anthropological study of an audiology clinic describes how American audiologists and otologists consistently proffer the image of signed languages taking over the brains of Deaf children (Fjord, 1999). For this group of professionals, the supposed damage that using a signed language inflicts on the brain causes "'visual areas to take over areas allocated to speech'" and "'neural atrophy of auditory path-ways'" (Fjord, p. 135). An Ontario Ministry of Health newsletter cites the "significant changes in the structural and functional organization of the auditory system, up to and including the cerebral cortex" that are caused by "auditory deprivation in early infancy" (Hyde, 2002, p. 176). This ominous view of hearing loss and signed language is connected to studies involving the brain scans of adult signed language users, which show signed languages stimulate brain substrates similarly to spoken languages (Fjord). Aphasias in the left hemisphere of the brain have also been shown to affect signed language grammar in the same way as these disorders affect spoken language grammar (Bellugi, 1980; Neville & Bellugi, 1978). Although these studies can be taken as evidence for the linguistic wholeness of signed languages, medical professionals and AVT advocates have focused on results showing the reallocation of auditory areas for visual processing in the brains of adult Deaf signed language users (Neville, 1988, 1991). The perceived effects of hearing loss and visual language on brain development become an argument for AVT where reliance on vision and signed language is prohibited. Hence, American and Canadian audiologists and otologists have not supported the concept of bilingual education in ASL and English for Deaf children.

Infant Hearing Screening and Early Intervention Programs

There is a general consensus that hearing loss in young children must be detected as early in life as possible to enable optimum access to language. Identification of hearing loss in infancy, followed by appropriate intervention by the age of 6 months, can result in normal language development (Anderson, 2006; Arehart & Yoshinaga-Itano, 1999; Schick, 2003; Yoshinaga-Itano, Sedey, Coulter, & Mehl, 1998). The 6-month deadline for intervention is supported by evidence from two large-scale studies of Deaf and hard of hearing infants in Colorado (Apuzzo & Yoshinaga-Itano, 1995; Yoshinaga-Itano et al., 1998). Children identified with hearing loss by 6 months of age have significantly higher receptive and expressive language skills than children with later-identified hearing loss. It has been proposed that age of identification does not directly result in improved speech production in Deaf children but instead positively influences language development (Yoshinaga-Itano, 2006). When children are able to produce lexical and grammatical units of language, regardless of modality, they have a framework for developing spoken-language articulation skills.

Prior to the technology introduced by universal hearing screening programs, the identification of Deaf and hard of hearing children was often delayed. Before the beginning of the 21st century, Deaf and hard of hearing children with hearing parents often had significant language delays before intervention services were initiated. The Ontario government established its Infant Hearing and Communication Development Program in May 2000 (Hyde, 2002). This endeavor followed a study that found that the mean age of diagnosis of hearing loss in Ontario between the years 1991–1995 was 2.8 years of age (Durieux-Smith & Whittingham, 2000). According to an article provided for orientation to the IHP, families with infants identified as having hearing loss "receive . . . evidence-based, unbiased information about communication development options" including "amplification, auditory-verbal therapy, sign language training, or a combined approach" (Hyde, Friedberg, Price, & Weber, 2004, p. 5).

However, there is a growing concern among researchers that many early intervention programs do not provide a well-informed or adequate range of options to parents and Deaf children. To address this gap, educators of Deaf and hard of hearing children with proficiency in signed language and understanding of the impact of hearing loss on language and socioemotional development must form an integral part of intervention systems (Arehart & Yoshinaga-Itano; Sass-Lehrer & Bodner-Johnson, 2003). A study by the Marion Downs National Center of 17 states with universal newborn hearing screening programs and intervention sites found only 30% of early intervention programs had an educator of Deaf children on staff (Arehart, Yoshinaga-Itano, Thomson, Gabbard, & Stredler-Brown, 1998). Similarly, another study noted that most early intervention programs do not provide any information about Deaf culture (Stredler-Brown & Arehart, 2000). Most early education providers for young Deaf children have backgrounds in speech-language pathology instead of Deaf education.

A systematic absence of Deaf education professionals and Deaf adults in infant hearing screening and early intervention systems has also been apparent among Ontario IHP administrators and staff members. A job opening for the manager of a local IHP coordinating agency stipulated a "Master's degree in Speech Pathology or Audiology" and "Current registration with the College of Speech Language Pathologists and Audiologists" as its chief qualifications. Yet training programs for speech-language pathologists and audiologists generally do not provide in-depth information about Deaf people or signed language. Such professionals can only be competent in the values that are transmitted to them by society and their training (Fjord, 1999). The otologists interviewed for one study stated that their training did not prepare them for working with Deaf people or provide any information about signed language (Fjord).

Cochlear Implants and Signed Language

The IHP's supposed options for Deaf infants and their families become a moot point when Ontario's children's hospital cochlear implant teams require families to provide AVT and thereby reject ASL for their child. Accordingly, the IHP has not funded ASL services to children receiving AVT. This prohibition on signed language for Deaf children with cochlear implants is part of the long history of a constructed binary opposition between spoken language and signed language by educators and medical professionals (Fjord, 1999). This opposition also represents a version of Cummins's separate underlying proficiency model, in which learning of a signed language is perceived to inhibit spoken English development. Yet the research presented in this chapter refutes this view.

Despite their broad implementation and public support, the efficacy of childhood cochlear implants and AVT for supporting first-language acquisition in Deaf children is inconclusive (Eriks-Brophy, 2004; Goldin-Meadow & Mayberry, 2001; Hyde, 2002; Spencer & Marschark, 2003). A review of studies evaluating AVT notes that this research tends to be retrospective and anecdotal in nature and is often based on a small, self-selected group of participants (Eriks-Brophy). This evidence would be classified as providing only limited support in favor of AVT as a treatment approach. Research on AVT also lacks a measure of these children's functioning across multiple domains, including social and emotional development. A longitudinal study of Deaf and hearing infants and parents found that mothers' use of signed language and gesture when children were 12 months old was strongly related to the infants' language progress, social interaction, and visual attention patterns at 18 months of age (Meadow-Orlans, Spencer, Koester, & Steinberg, 2004). These writers conclude that strict adherence to an auditory-verbal regimen that decreases visual input is likely to delay the overall language and social development of children with a hearing loss, especially those whose loss is severe or profound.

Although cochlear implants can improve access to sound and speech perception and production (Blamey, 2003; Blamey et al., 2001; Preisler et al., 2002), their performance is not uniform. The outcomes of cochlear implants in young Deaf children have been described as "uneven and unpredictable" (Meadow-Orlans et al., 2004, p. 219). Cochlear implants also do not transform a Deaf child into a hearing one. Most Deaf children with cochlear implants are functionally hard of hearing (Blamey, 2003; Blamey et al., 2001; Schick et al., 2006; Spencer, 2002; Spencer & Marschark,

2003), and hard of hearing children face severe developmental, communication and educational difficulties (Blamey, 2003; Preisler, 1999; Preisler & Ahlström, 1997; Schick et al., 2006). One study of 87 primary school children found the average rate of spoken language development for children with hearing aids and cochlear implants was about 55% of the rate for normal spoken language development in hearing children (Blamey et al., 2001). This author also states that "a hard of hearing child has about 40%–60% of the learning opportunities of a hearing child" due to limited auditory experiences, and as a consequence his or her "learning rate is about 40%–60% of normal" (Blamey, 2003, p. 241).

The social and emotional development of hard of hearing children is similarly affected. It has been reported that both Deaf and hard of hearing children interact less frequently with hearing peers, spend less time in interaction, and engage in briefer interactions than hearing children owing to more limited spoken language abilities (Antia & Kreimeyer, 2003). Other researchers found that a study group of hard of hearing children aged between 2 and 7 lacked knowledge of rules for communication including turn-taking and making eye contact (Preisler & Ahlström, 1997).

Hard of hearing children and Deaf children with cochlear implants also benefit from exposure to a signed language. Perhaps especially for this group of children with some hearing abilities, acquiring a signed language early in childhood can benefit spoken language development in significant ways. Case studies have been conducted of infants involved with the Colorado Home Intervention Program who acquired ASL and simultaneously received cochlear implants and auditory-oral stimulation (Yoshinaga-Itano, 2006). These young children's broad ASL vocabularies were a foundation for developing spoken English word perception and production skills.

A model for simultaneous bilingualism in ASL and English for Deaf children with cochlear implants can be envisioned in which individual proficiency and progress in spoken language may still be varied, however. Some of the most compelling evidence for this model comes from a longitudinal study of Swedish Deaf children with cochlear implants (Preisler, Tvingstedt, & Ahlström, 2002, 2005). These researchers interviewed 11 children aged between 8.5 and 10.5 with cochlear implants about their experiences (Preisler et al., 2005). At the time of the follow-up 2005 study, the children had been using their implants for 5.0 to 7.5 years. Six of these children attended schools for the Deaf and five were in mainstream classes. Owing to the Swedish model of Deaf education, in which signed language has been the official language of instruction since 1981, these children and their families used Swedish sign language in addition to spoken language. In the earlier study, parents used mainly signed language with their young children and introduced more spoken language as time passed (Preisler et al., 2002). In the 2005 study results, children enrolled at schools for Deaf students expressed no difficulty in understanding what was said in the classroom environment. However, children in mainstream classrooms where spoken Swedish was used reported more difficulties in understanding their teacher and in communication in a group environment. This observation was consistent with their parents' and teachers' comments. With impaired hearing, it is more difficult to create meaning and coherence from spoken language utterances. The study authors expressed concern regarding the students' need to develop linguistic competence for the increasing abstraction in higher education. Mainstream classroom environments that do not provide exposure to signed language may not support the fluency needed for full linguistic competence.

Preisler and colleagues' (2005) description of the difficulties that a mainstream classroom environment poses for Deaf children with cochlear implants is corroborated by researchers in other countries (e.g., Knecht, Nelson, Whitelaw, & Feth, 2002; Shield & Dockrell, 2004). These researchers report that even when children with cochlear implants are able to hear within normal limits for some situations, the noise levels in most classrooms are too high to enable easy understanding of speech. Although excessive noise levels and high reverberation in the classroom can negatively impact the performance of hearing children, children with hearing loss are most at risk for having difficulty in noisy classrooms (Picard & Bradley, 2001).

Early ASL Intervention

Because hearing parents of Deaf children may often not begin learning a signed language until after their child's hearing loss has been identified, it is sometimes argued that these children lack access to fluent first-language models and as a consequence may be delayed in their acquisition of signed language, as well as spoken/written language. Initiatives proposed by the Deaf community, however, have focused on the involvement of Deaf adults as language models for Deaf children and their families. Involving ASL-proficient Deaf adult professionals in early intervention and education programs facilitates opportunities for language-based interaction, language play, and sharing ASL literature with young Deaf children. Successful models for this type of program have been established in Canada and the United States (Roberts, 1998; Watkins et al., 1998).

One group of researchers reported on a groundbreaking Deaf Mentor Experimental Project in Utah, in which Deaf adults made regular home visits to young Deaf children and their families to share their knowledge of ASL and Deaf culture and serve as role models (Watkins et al., 1998). The group of Deaf children receiving Deaf mentor services was matched to a control group of children and parents in Tennessee who received only spoken or manually coded English services. Average receptive and expressive language gains for the Utah children were 6 months greater than those for the Tennessee control group. Moreover, the Utah children with exposure to ASL scored more than 2.5 times higher on a test of English grammar than the Tennessee children. Parents reported that children in the Utah Deaf Mentor program had vocabularies more than twice the size of the matched children in Tennessee, and parents themselves knew and used more than six times as many signs as the parents in Tennessee.

A Deaf Mentor and Outreach ASL Program at the Sir James Whitney School for the Deaf in Belleville, Ontario, was begun in 1993 to provide services to families on the preschool home visiting caseload (Roberts, 1998). The Deaf community organization that is described in this book began its ASL and Early Literacy Consultant Program in 2001 with the goal of developing province-wide standards and training for Deaf family ASL instructors and ASL and early literacy resources for parents and children. In 2002, the Ontario IHP provided this organization with 3 years of start-up funding to assist with training, materials development, and referrals for ASL and early literacy consultants. However, funding for this infrastructure ceased in March 2005. The IHP coordinating agencies still contract family ASL instructors to assist families who request ASL services. However, bilingual ASL and English programs and services have not been consistently supported by the IHP. As a result, few families with young Deaf children in Ontario access ASL services.

The ASL Parent-Child Mother Goose Program

The Parent-Child Mother Goose Program began in 1984 as a pilot program in Toronto for parents and children identified by the Children's Aid Society as being socially disadvantaged. In 1986, the program was extended to include families in the general community. The program focuses on the use of spoken language rhymes, rhythms, and stories to nurture the parent–child relationship. No toys, books, or other props are used, although parents have reported that their use of oral rhymes and songs strengthens and complements reading books with their children (Canadian Institute of Child Health, 2001). There is research showing the spoken language program's efficacy in promoting positive parent–child interaction, family well-being, and English literacy (e.g., Canadian Institute of Child Health). This research also mentions the program's use with parents and children who are learning English as a second language.

Like the original program, the ASL Parent-Child Mother Goose Program features ASL literature as a form of oral literature (Bahan, 1991). ASL rhymes, rhythms, and stories are used, with ASL rhymes being formed through the repetition of handshapes, movement paths of signs, or nonmanual signals (Bauman, 2003; Valli, 1990). ASL rhythms involve recurring and patterned motions in ASL poems. Because many ASL rhymes also involve rhythm, and vice versa, throughout this book I will use the term "ASL rhyme" to refer to the short ASL poems used in the ASL Parent-Child Mother Goose Program.

In young Deaf children, language play—including signed games, rhythmic signing activities, and simple ASL poetry—is linked to the development of metalinguistic awareness, which in hearing children typically emerges during the preschool years (Erting & Pfau, 1997; Snow et al., 1998). Shared rhymes and stories also develop language skills that are precursors to print literacy in young children. With its focus on ASL handshape rhymes and stories, the ASL Parent-Child Mother Goose Program promotes awareness of ASL phonology and the development of a broad ASL vocabulary akin to the spoken English vocabulary developed by hearing children's use of nursery rhymes. Rhymes and storytelling also facilitate children's familiarity with the structural organization of literature (Heath, 1983; Snow et al., 1998). In view of its potential to enhance Deaf children's first-language literacy in ASL, and in light of the demonstrated relationship between ASL proficiency and English literacy in Deaf students, this program can be viewed as a support for emergent literacy in both ASL and English.

The factors that contribute to young children's reading success include oral language proficiency and opportunities for verbal interaction. The ASL Parent-Child Mother Goose Program encourages parents to use ASL rhymes and rhythms with their children at home and elsewhere. In addition, parental attitudes about literacy are often conveyed to children during the preschool years. Participation in the program can play a role in shaping parents' attitudes toward early literacy in ASL, and by participating in a shared family early ASL literary program, parents can convey to their children that ASL literacy and literature are necessary and valued. As ASL literature is often the most accessible literature for young Deaf children, the promotion of an ASL literature tradition and enhanced communication between parents and children can be seen as important functions of a family ASL literacy program.

3 Discourse and Counterdiscourse

As a system of being, a *discourse* concerns itself with particular matters and promotes certain ideas, perspectives, and values at the expense of others. In doing so, a given discourse will marginalize perspectives and values that are central to other discourses. Or, as Foucault (1972) argues, "Discourses . . . systematically form the objects of which they speak" (p. 39). Some writers have explored historical representations of and discourses surrounding Deaf people that are linked to social and educational practices and structures that render Deaf people as disabled instead of a distinct linguistic minority (e.g., Ladd, 2003; Lane, 1992). The construction of Deaf people as disabled often serves to channel Deaf students away from bilingual education programs and socialization with the Deaf community and toward habilitation via the practices of oralism (Komesaroff, 2008; Lane, 1992; Lane et al., 1996). In this regard, medical and educational discourses surrounding Deaf identity bear similarities to discourses opposing bilingual education for hearing children on the grounds that language and cultural differences are deficiencies (Cummins, 2001).

Deaf People as Involuntary Minorities

John Ogbu (1992) devised the categories of voluntary and involuntary minorities as a way to approach the academic underachievement of certain groups of students as compared with others. *Voluntary minorities* are groups of people who have arrived in another society of their own accord in hopes of better economic prospects, more opportunities, and/or greater freedom than they found in their own countries. Because of the volun-

28

tary nature of their minority status in the new society, Ogbu argues, the "primary cultural differences" that voluntary minority students carry do not cause as many problems in school. These unique aspects of voluntary minority students' home cultures and languages were in existence before the students' arrival and did not develop as a means of opposition to or protection from the majority culture. Since these primary cultural differences are not seen as being in competition with mainstream society, voluntary minorities tend to approach school and second language learning more willingly and encounter fewer problems than involuntary minorities. In other words, voluntary minorities do not buck the system.

Involuntary minorities, on the other hand, are groups of people who were brought into another society against their will through "slavery, conquest, colonization, or forced labour" (Ogbu, 1992, p. 8). Deaf culture theorists have argued for the view of Deaf people as a colonized minority, particularly in terms of linguistic and cultural colonialism, and it is in these terms that I regard Deaf people as an involuntary minority group. Assigned an inferior status, involuntary minorities have also been denied opportunities to truly integrate with the majority culture and as a consequence, developed "secondary cultural differences to cope with their subordination" (Ogbu, p. 8). These secondary cultural differences have a greater impact on the educational experiences of involuntary minorities in part because these differences appear to be associated with an oppositional collective identity versus a mainstream, dominant-culture social identity. According to Ogbu, voluntary minorities appear to bring a sense of identity with them from their homeland and retain this identity (which is different from, but not in opposition to, majority culture). However, involuntary minorities appear to develop a new collective identity after their subordination "that is in opposition to the social identity of the dominant group" (Ogbu, p. 9). This new identity is a response to their treatment by the dominant group "in economic, political, social, psychological, cultural, and language domains" (Ogbu, p. 9).

Secondary cultural differences cause problems in school for involuntary minorities because these differences "evolved as coping mechanisms" under conditions of oppression, and involuntary minorities have little incentive to give up these cultural differences "as long as they believe they are still oppressed" (Ogbu, 1992, p. 10). These differences between involuntary minority and mainstream students in communication, cognitive, interactional, or learning styles result in the perception by involuntary minorities that school success entails "acting white." In other words, Ogbu argues, school learning can be viewed as a process that is detrimental to involuntary minorities' "social identity, sense of security, and self-worth" (p. 10). If involuntary minorities acquire a majority-culture frame of reference, then they fear that they may cease acting like involuntary minorities and lose their identity, sense of community, and feelings of self-worth. Furthermore, writes Ogbu, it has been demonstrated that involuntary minorities who "learn to 'act white' or who succeed in school are not fully accepted" by the dominant culture and never receive opportunities or rewards that are equal to those available to members of the dominant group with a similar education (p. 10). In addition, those involuntary minority students who are perceived as "acting white" run the risk of ostracism from their home community: Such students "usually experience isolation" from other involuntary minority students, "resulting in high psychological costs" (Ogbu, p. 11).

In the case of orally educated Deaf students, there is a phenomenon of cultural homelessness that is similar to the plight of academically successful involuntary minority students (Lane, 1992). According to this argument, when Deaf students leave their "oral programs of home and school, they find that the hearing world no longer sees these students as superior to signing deaf adults" and that many hearing people are unused to the speech of orally educated Deaf people (Lane, 1992, p. 288). Many of these students choose to learn ASL; however, when they do, they may face a negative reaction from their parents. Turning to the Deaf community for support, orally educated Deaf students may experience discrimination in reverse. "Gunned down by both sides, some young oral Deaf people may refuse to take either side" and as a consequence, lose connection with the social world (Lane, p. 288).

In a first-hand account of cultural homelessness, Jill Jones (2003) recounted her experiences as a former mainstreamed Deaf student attempting to join the Deaf community as an adult:

> I visited Deaf clubs, met Deaf people, but still no joy. I was seen as a J who could speak, not a J who was Deaf. I took signing classes to see if this helped. I could sign but thought this may help. No way. As the years went by I tried everything but nothing worked. I could not fully enjoy the world of the hearing as I could not hear well. Nor could I fully enjoy the world of the Deaf. (p. 16)

In the present day, these perceived reservations on the Deaf community's part toward welcoming orally educated individuals may have been partly relaxed due to the fact that the numbers of mainstreamed Deaf students—many of whom lack access to signed language—by far outstrip the numbers of students who attended Deaf residential schools. Or at least, there are now enough orally educated Deaf students and former students to form a subgroup of their own.

However, it may be more difficult to tie Ogbu's theories regarding involuntary minorities to the academic success of Deaf students (apart from spoken-language proficiency—in Deaf education, the two concepts are frequently conflated), given that signed language skills in themselves are often the best predictors of overall academic performance. In addition, learning and knowledge are highly valued by the Deaf community where Deaf individuals often take on the role of teaching each other: "The trope of 'information' is . . . a highly significant Deaf cultural value" (Ladd, 2003, p. 353). An anecdote about the pre-1970s

German Deaf community is cited: "'It always struck me that there was such thirst for knowledge among the Deaf. They longed for more information and sat together until late in the night to share information. This is a typical feature of their culture'" (Ladd, p. 146). It is also sometimes difficult to apply the concept of secondary as opposed to primary cultural differences in the case of Deaf students, because enduring hallmarks of Deaf culture like the valuation of native signed languages predate modern-day medical and educational discourses. Signed languages and Deaf culture did not spring up in opposition to oralism, although oppression may have strengthened the Deaf community's self-awareness, convictions, and cultural beliefs as well as its resistance to some facets of dominant, spoken-language cultures.

Viewing minority status and schooling in a Canadian context, Jim Cummins (1997) highlights some difficulties with broadly applying Ogbu's theories to diverse groups of students. Rather, writes Cummins, student underachievement is better viewed from within the framework of relations of power in the classroom where educators as well as students play a crucial role in negotiating identities. When the exercise of power by a dominant entity takes on the quality of coercion, a process of definition takes place whereby the identities of minority students are further stigmatized and the superior status of the dominant group is affirmed. These coercive relations of power both reflect and produce dominant-culture discourses. For example, Cummins outlines the history of residential schools for aboriginal students in Canada, where a "process of destruction of identity" took place (p. 418). As he writes, "The negotiation of identity in educational contexts is a mutual process" (p. 418). In order for educators of First Nations children "to define their roles as bearers of salvation, civilization and education," the teachers had to simultaneously define these students as "savage and ignorant" (p. 418). This educational discourse surrounding First Nations students in Canada, like all other discourses, is a product of history (Gee,

2008). Educators of aboriginal students who participated in this dual process of identity definition were channels for historically and socially defined discourses that "speak to each other through individuals" (Gee, p. 162). The historic role of residential schools for Deaf students, however, is in some ways distinct from the history and function of Canadian residential schools for First Nations students. The schools for Deaf students were the sites for transmission of signed language and Deaf culture.

This dual process of identity definition and activation of dominant discourses also takes place in oralist education of Deaf students, where "educators of deaf pupils believe the most negative claims about signed language" despite linguistic evidence to the contrary because these teachers' concept of Deaf students "requires deaf people's linguistic and intellectual inferiority" (Lane, 1992, pp. 46–47). In sum, Deaf students are seen as "intellectually deficient . . . because they lack true language" (Lane, p. 47). It is "the ethnocentrism of paternalism" (p. 47) that explains the persistence of educators of Deaf students' irrational beliefs and pedagogical practices such as signed English. Put another way, pathologizing discourses regarding Deaf children and adults cannot recognize the validity of signed language and Deaf culture because doing so would challenge the very foundations of those discourses.

In addition to presenting a more comprehensive framework for viewing minority student achievement within the context of societal power relations, Cummins's concept of dual identity negotiation between student and teacher avoids more problematic aspects of Ogbu's arguments. Ogbu acknowledges that "schools themselves appear to approach the education of involuntary students defensively through strategies of control and paternalism which divert attention from efforts to educate minority children" (1993, p. 103). However, his focus on involuntary minority students' interpretations and responses to these strategies that render the students "more or less accomplices to their own school success or failure" (1993, p. 88) has the troubling appearance of blaming the victim.

More to the point, Ogbu's emphasis on student complicity and responsibility appears to focus more on changing students' ways to accommodate and assimilate to the system than on challenging larger power structures that are at the root of oppression. For instance, it is frequently claimed that the values embedded in a minority discourse may play a role in reproducing minority students' and their parents place near "the bottom of the social hierarchy," because resistance to school values will lead to a lack of academic success and thus fewer opportunities (Gee, 2008, p. 193). However, such observations obscure the fact that minority students realize schools as they stand "will never accept and value their community's social practices and never give that community, on a full and fair basis, access to dominant secondary discourses" and the social goods that accompany them (Gee, p. 193).

There is also a positive side to involuntary minority students' resistance of dominant-culture norms and expectations by holding fast to their own culture's values. By expressing their authentic identities in their own "voices," students can render themselves "visible" and the authors of their own worlds (Ellsworth, 1989, p. 309). This self-definition allows minority students a space where they can act as agents of social and political change. Such a process of self-definition is also crucial to the identity and agency of the Deaf community. Although hearing people may believe that Deaf people's goal is to be included in mainstream society, "it is more likely that Deaf people's goal is one of maintenance of boundaries between cultures and a search for accommodation that allows the Deaf person to remain true to the self" (T. Humphries, cited in McKee, 2008, p. 532). Due to ongoing efforts to "normalize" Deaf children, there is likely to be anger in the Deaf community (Emery, 2003). This anger can be channelled in many directions, including the positive direction of political protest. Like political protest, the authentic voices of minority students often appear insubordinate in nature, for such students do not simply share information regarding the oppression that conditions their lives. Rather, the expressions of minority students are a kind of "talking back" and defiance "that is constructed within communities of resistance and is a condition of survival" (Ellsworth, p. 310).

As well as serving a process of self-definition, minority students' resistance of dominant academic discourses has benefits for critical thinking. Resistance to such discourses is also resistance to literacy for dominant cultural reproduction, which "uses institutional mechanisms to undermine independent thought" (Macedo, 1993, p. 186). From this perspective, the academic underachievers among us come out on top because "the less educated one is, in the reproductive dominant model, the greater the chances to read the world more critically" (Macedo, p. 203). Further arguments have been made for the advantage that comes from having failed to fully master dominant-culture discourses. When minority students find themselves in situations where they are unable to accommodate or adapt to mainstream discourses, they acquire a conscious awareness of and deeper insight into what they are trying to do (Gee, 2008). This insight or "meta-knowledge" can enable students "to manipulate the society where a given discourse is dominant," if students also have access to a "liberating literacy"—a theory of society and the student's position in it—that forms "a basis for resistance to oppression" (Gee, p. 180).

In addition, the concept of discourses allows for fluidity and social change, because every time an individual acts within a given discourse or discourses, he or she can also act to change or re-create those discourses: "If you pull off a performance and it gets 'recognized' as meaningful and appropriate in the discourse, then it 'counts.' That performance carries, like a virus, aspects of your own individuality and, too, of your other discourses" (Gee,

p. 195). An ASL discourse, like other minority, community-based discourses, can contain the seeds of liberation from dominant discourses. This ASL discourse can act as "a form of self-defence against colonization"; like all organized resistance to power, such an ASL discourse is not always successful, but neither does it always fail (Gee, p. 193).

Research as Praxis

4

As I PLANNED my participatory action research study of the ASL Parent-Child Mother Goose Program, I considered several factors. One of these factors was the pervasiveness of systemic barriers to young Deaf children and their families' learning of ASL in an Ontario early intervention context. This issue over-shadowed my study's planning and execution in more ways than I originally predicted. I therefore sought to extend my role as ethnographer to that of "a change agent who is collaboratively developing structures intended to critique and support the trans-formation of the communities being studied" (Barab, Thomas, Dodge, Squire, & Newell, 2004, p. 255). An action research meth-odology seemed to best embody Freire's (2000) concept of *praxis,* in which participants' dialogue and reflection occur in tandem with intervention for transformation of their world.

Both action research and participant observation require the re-searcher to be actively involved in the study. Therefore, a primary concern for my study was balancing participant interests: I had to balance an understanding of my own agenda and my subjectivity as a researcher with a commitment to understanding participants' own perspectives and goals (Barab et al., 2004). To support the democratic and collegial environment demanded by action re-search, I had to foster communication between the participants and myself (Cohen, Manion, & Morrison, 2000). Commitment to dialogue and reflexivity on my part, and a willingness to revise the research agenda were needed in order to balance the program design with principles of action research.

I chose the ASL Parent-Child Mother Goose Program for my study of Deaf and hearing children and parents, in part for reasons of access. The lack of support for ASL services in Ontario at the time of my study meant that few sites existed in which I could study young Deaf children and their parents' ASL literacy practices. In the year 2005, just as its funding and infrastructure for overseeing ASL services terminated, the local Deaf community organization (DCO) received a new, 3-year foundation grant for ASL Parent-Child Mother Goose Program provider training and materials development. This funding provided the means for the organization's family ASL literacy program to continue and expand, even in the absence of the previous infrastructure for ASL services.

Research Setting

My study took place at a Deaf service agency (DSA) in the province of Ontario, where local parents with young Deaf children are often referred by a regional Ontario IHP coordinating agency. DSA hosts a biweekly drop-in center for parents and children, and aims at promoting a neutral perspective on the contested domain of language choice for Deaf children. Neither ASL nor AVT is advocated, although agency staff members state that ASL is part of the drop-in center environment and AVT services are offered on-site. The drop-in center is open to parents with Deaf children up to the age of 6. DSA also hosts a preschool for Deaf children and hearing children of Deaf parents, in addition to a number of early-years programs.

Ethical considerations arose as I planned my study, owing to the characteristics of the participant group of Deaf children with hearing parents. I anticipated that at least some of the children in this group would have cochlear implants and/or be enrolled in AVT. I also anticipated some concern on these families' part that their enrollment with AV therapists would be threatened if it were disclosed that their children were participating in an ASL literature program. However, ASL users were already present in DSA as staff members and clients, and so ASL was part of the DSA environment before our program took place. Our program was offered as a complimentary addition to DSA's resources for parents of Deaf children.

I had previously worked with the ASL Parent-Child Mother Goose Program Coordinator (who was also our program leader) during participant observation of an 8-week program in the fall of 2005. Whereas the fall 2005 program involved hearing parents with hearing children, for my present study I planned for a participant group of mainly hearing parents and young Deaf children, but several issues prevented me from accessing my group of initial choice. In the urban center that was the setting for my study—located in the same city as one of the children's hospitals with prohibitions on learning ASL—not many hearing parents of young Deaf children choose ASL as an IHP service option. In the beginning, I faced the prospect of not being able to find any participants for my study. Additionally, the children's program at DSA where our program was held is intended to be accessible to all Deaf and hearing parents of Deaf and hard of hearing children. Because our program was being advertised and hosted by DSA, it was important for us to be open to all parents registered with the agency who wished to participate.

Because both Deaf and hearing parents participated in our program, the different roles and contributions of these parents became central research issues. I chose to focus on both groups of parents' experiences in and contributions to the program in the overall context of Ontario infant hearing screening and early intervention services. In addition, the child participants ranged in age from 4 to 11 months at the beginning of our program, and had varying degrees of exposure to ASL. Because the child participants were so young, I decided to focus on emergent ASL

literacy. The goals of the program leader and the issue of public resources were also viewed in the context of Ontario infant
hearing screening and early intervention services.

During the 8-week time period when our program was held,
I also attended several related events, including a family event
hosted by DSA and DCO's annual general meeting. I also met
with the program leader and DSA staff outside of our program
to follow up with themes that had emerged during my research
and with administrative issues related to our program.

Data Collection

In observing and recording all participants in addition to my own
actions and experiences during the program, I employed multiple methods of qualitative data gathering in concurrent phases:
open-ended and structured observations, semistructured and
focus group interviews, and a document review.

I used field notes and videotaping of programs for observations. The video data of each program session enabled me to
further observe and analyze the program in addition to many of
the interviews. The detailed field notes that I took during and immediately following each program session recorded the themes of
child participants' visual attention, response, and use of language
play and the parent participants' independent use and improvisations of ASL rhymes, in addition to other themes that emerged. I
also took field notes during and after the DSA family event and
DCO board of directors' meeting that I observed.

I conducted interviews in both ASL and English. An ASL interpreter was present for the duration of the 8-week program to
allow free and easy communication between Deaf and hearing
parents and the Deaf program leader and researcher. I recorded
interview data via field notes and video camera, translated interviews into English (from the ASL video data), and transcribed
them for further analysis. The initial, semistructured interviews

that I conducted with parent participants were aimed at exploring the extent of parents and children's previous experience with ASL, ASL literature, and other types of early intervention services. I also conducted semistructured, follow-up interviews with the program leader at the end of each program session and outside of our program. These interviews enabled me to explore and clarify the program leader's teaching goals, observations, and perspectives on various issues. Discussions that focused on parents' use of ASL rhymes at home and childrens' response took the form of focus group interviews led by the program leader. At the beginning of each program session, he reviewed each parent participant's progress with using ASL rhymes and stories and asked how their child had responded. In addition, over the course of our program several group discussions took place about issues relating to Deaf culture, hearing loss, and hearing technology.

My review of Parent-Child Mother Goose Program and ASL Parent-Child Mother Goose Program training and resource materials enabled me to gather data regarding program objectives and compare the support and resources that were respectively available to the spoken-language and ASL programs.

All qualitative data was transcribed and organized thematically by a set of coding schemes. I categorized the data into themes: the issue of available resources for Deaf and hearing parents, the impact of gatekeepers, child response to ASL rhymes and stories, comparisons made by participants between hearing and Deaf people and perspectives on Deaf identity, name signs, the roles of Deaf and hearing mothers, the program leader's goals and role, and suggestions for improvements to the program.

Participants

Six families signed up for our program: two with Deaf parents and Deaf children, one with a Deaf parent and hearing child, and

Table 4.1. Individual Family Composition

Child's name	Child's age at start of program	Child's identity as described by parent(s)	Parent(s)' name(s)	Parent(s)' identity
Charlie	7 months	Hard of hearing/Deaf	Bianca	Hearing
David	9 months	Deaf	Grace	Hearing
Henry	4 months	Deaf	Julia	Deaf
Sarah	11 months	Deaf	Mary and Peter	Deaf
Thomas	5 months	Hard of hearing	Alison	Hearing
Violet	6 months	Hearing	Donna	Deaf

three with hearing parents and Deaf or hard of hearing children. Each family or mother/child dyad who participated became a miniature case study. Attendance was most regular for four of the families, and two attended more sporadically. Data regarding the families' makeup is presented in Table 4.1.

Parent and Child Participants

Charlie and Bianca. Charlie and his mother Bianca attended our program regularly.[1] At the first session, Bianca reported that Charlie had a "moderate to severe" hearing loss. However, during the course of our program, Bianca mentioned that Charlie was referred for repeated hearing tests, and it appeared that he had a more severe hearing loss than originally thought—from a severe to profound loss. Bianca and Charlie were referred to DSA (which informed Bianca about the ASL Parent-Child Mother Goose Program) by the IHP. In a preliminary interview, Bianca reported having attended one AVT session with Charlie, and told me she planned to access ASL and literacy consultant services. (It later came to light that Bianca had originally requested dual-language services that included learning ASL, but had instead been referred to AVT services by the IHP.) She also said that our program was the first time she and Charlie had gotten involved with learning ASL, although she has a Sign With Your Baby kit

---

1. All participant names (except for my own) are pseudonyms.

at home and had registered for, but not yet started, a baby sign program for hearing parents and children.

David and Grace. David and his mother Grace attended three program sessions. Grace had arrived in Canada from Hungary four years earlier, and Hungarian was her own and David's first language. Grace learned about DSA through the IHP and was invited to attend our program when she met the program leader, Jonathan, at DSA's family event. David attended weekly AVT sessions, and Grace reported that our ASL Parent-Child Mother Goose Program was the first time she and David were exposed to learning ASL.

Henry and Julia. Henry and his mother Julia attended every program session. Julia first learned about DSA services for parents with young Deaf children from a DSA staff member. Julia is a social worker and ASL instructor and is trained as an ASL and literacy consultant and ASL Parent-Child Mother Goose Program leader. She and Henry received ASL and literacy consultant services on a weekly basis, through the IHP.

Sarah, Mary, and Peter. Sarah and her parents Mary and Peter attended two sessions. This family had arrived in Canada five months earlier as refugees from Mexico, and their native language is Mexican sign language, or Lengua de señas mexicana (LSM). Peter previously attended Gallaudet University where he learned ASL, and Mary worked as a teacher of Deaf children in Mexico. Mary and Peter learned about the ASL Parent-Child Mother Goose Program from a friend. They reported receiving dual language (ASL and auditory-oral) services from the IHP.

Thomas and Alison. Thomas (Tom) and his mother Alison attended our program regularly. Tom was reported to have a unilateral (in one ear), severe hearing loss. They were referred to our program by the IHP and did not receive other services.

Violet and Donna. Violet and her mother Donna attended our program regularly. Donna learned about the DSA program from a family member who was also an IHP employee. Donna's family background is Chinese-Canadian, and her hearing relatives speak Chinese in addition to English with Violet. Donna is a kindergarten teacher at a provincial school for Deaf students and is trained as an ASL Parent-Child Mother Goose Program leader.

The ASL Parent-Child Mother Goose Program Leader

At the time of the study, the program leader, Jonathan, was one of only two certified trainers of ASL Parent-Child Mother Goose Program leaders (having received training and certification from the founders of the Parent-Child Mother Goose Program). Jonathan is a senior ASL and literacy consultant and a university ASL instructor. He also teaches ASL in community college and service agency settings.

Jonathan's role in my study as a key agent and action-taker was crucial for co-constructing (along with the other Deaf adult participants) a Deaf cultural space in which an ASL discourse was embodied. Through his guidance of our collective action and dialogue, Jonathan's participation illustrated both the importance of collaboration to action research and how the tension among a range of participant perspectives, common to action research, emerged and was resolved.

Researcher as Participant

At our program's first session, Jonathan introduced me to the other participants as a former program coordinator for DCO (where he was now employed as ASL Parent-Child Mother Goose Program Coordinator). I also told the participants that I was a PhD student. While I mentioned other aspects of my background and identity in passing during our program—such as the fact that, unlike the other Deaf adults present, I grew up attending mainstream schools where I was the only Deaf student—I did not disclose everything that might have become a point of interest to the hearing adult participants. For instance, I did not share the fact that I had received a cochlear implant when I was 15, or that I had stopped using it after 4 years. This was partly because I did not want curiosity about my experiences to overshadow our program or influence participants' perceptions of my role and agenda as a researcher. However, because I am a member of the Deaf community and a former colleague of several Deaf participants, these latter aspects of my background and identity were known by the Deaf adults in my study.

As a Deaf late second-language learner of ASL, I agree with the notion of social identity as a site of struggle and as multiple and contradictory (Norton Peirce, 1995, p.15). Although learning ASL and claiming membership in the Deaf community have greatly enriched my adult life, neither process has been brief or free of difficulty. My multiple, contradictory social identity, as well as my professional experience, has given me a window on the perspectives of not only other Deaf individuals, but also of other bilingual ASL and English learners and educators, and of Deaf and hearing parents of Deaf children. As befits an action research study, I make no claims to neutrality or disinterestedness in my position as researcher. Instead, my approach to the subject of ASL and early literacy is one of critical inquiry, which, as Maria José Botelho writes, "is an open space for people to take risks and learn from each other, knowing that our take on the world is partial. This partiality is shaped by how we are privileged and targeted by our social identities" (2006, personal communication). The diversity among participants in my study—including hearing and Deaf adults, and first- and second-language learners of ASL—meant that such an open space for risk-taking was possible. Throughout my study, there were several instances when I was compelled to revisit my prior assumptions about other participants and their respective interests, and reexamine my own agenda as a researcher.

The Role of the ASL Interpreter

Our ASL interpreter played a crucial role in facilitating communication between the Deaf and hearing participants in our program and making the program's use of ASL literature more accessible to the participants who were ASL learners. The interpreter whom I chose for my study is highly skilled and experienced and is certified by both federal- and provincial-level signed language interpreting associations. During my study, the interpreter occasionally approached me to discuss her role in communicative situations involving hearing parents who lacked significant experience with learning ASL. For some of these situations, she added certain information about the meaning and structure of ASL words, and she intervened by telling Jonathan or myself when hearing parents needed additional help with learning ASL rhymes. In these situations, the interpreter was conscious of having potentially overstepped her role and of relying on her own judgment of when it was appropriate to intervene. However, I felt that in discussing the issue with me, the interpreter and I reached a better understanding of our practice and shared interests. A proactive approach on the interpreter's part also seemed appropriate for an action research study aimed at fostering collaboration and practical outcomes.

ASL as Resource

5

A language is worth what those who speak it are worth.
                                             —Pierre Bourdieu

THE ISSUE OF public resources for supporting the learning of ASL by Deaf children is central to this book. Every aspect of our program—its hosting, duration, participants, and setting—was affected by the lack of financial and institutional support from governments and public bodies for teaching and learning ASL.

Even with its new foundation grant for program leader training and program expansion, DCO faced obstacles to hosting its family ASL literacy program. Like the spoken-language Parent-Child Mother Goose Program, the ASL program is intended to be run by two program leaders in a setting provided by a hosting agency or organization. Especially when program participants include hearing parents, the costs for hosting an ASL Parent-Child Mother Goose Program include the fees for service of two trained, ASL-proficient program leaders and an ASL interpreter. There is no cost to parents for participating in either the spoken-language or ASL Parent-Child Mother Goose Program, so program expenses must be covered by a hosting agency.

One potential hosting agency was the Ontario Early Years Centres. Under the jurisdiction of the Ontario Ministry of Children and Youth Services and funded by the Ontario government, the Ontario Early Years Centres are public sites for caregivers and children aged 0–6 to access early language and literacy programs and other resources (Ministry of Children & Youth Services, 2010). Jonathan had sent out letters to all Ontario Early Years Centre managers in the province asking if they were interested in hosting a program, which carried a cost of approximately $2,000, and received no positive response. Ontario Early Years Centres managers did, however, respond with significant interest to a second letter Jonathan sent out, in which DCO offered to pay the costs of hosting programs. DCO was therefore obliged to cover all costs of hosting programs at various locations in Ontario. This obligation meant that a smaller number of programs were held than was originally planned, and several newly trained program leaders lacked opportunities to use their skills. For our program at DSA, and for several others that he informed me about and that I saw advertised in flyers and emails, Jonathan as an organization employee was the only program leader. Although the Ministry of Children and Youth Services' (2010) website claims that the Ontario Early Years Centres provide services to children with special needs, it appears that budgetary constraints have dictated that early ASL literacy resources are not widely available.

The lack of resources for ASL parents and children also affected our program space at DSA. Whereas our first three program sessions were held in the main room of the building that houses DSA's drop-in center, due to other events taking place at DSA, our program had moved to a much smaller room in the same building by the 4th week. The agency regularly rents out its space for private events such as weddings that are often unrelated to the Deaf community. Even when we returned to the larger room for the 6th and 8th weeks of our program, physical evidence of these private events remained. On one occasion, the room was crowded with various pieces of furniture from a recent event and on another occasion, folding chairs were stacked in a rear corner. During our 6th program session, the wooden floor was dirty from a recent, private event and there was a brief upset when it appeared that Charlie had swallowed some debris.

A further obstacle DCO faced related to finding participants for the ASL Parent-Child Mother Goose Program. Even after the organization contacted several Ontario Early Years Centres and made arrangements to hold programs, center staff had to cancel some programs due to low numbers of registrants. For example, during the course of our program at DSA it was announced that Julia, who is also a trained program leader, would be leading her own program in an eastern Ontario town, but there were not enough registrants. The widespread prohibition that AVT practitioners placed on Deaf children's learning of ASL meant that a main target population for both my study and the program—Deaf children and hearing parents—was difficult to access. In addition, the numbers of Deaf parents with hearing or Deaf children who may also be interested in attending a program are relatively small. These constraints on funding and difficulties with finding participants also meant that the program featured in my study was only 8 weeks in length, as compared to the 30 weeks, or three 10-week programs spaced out over the course of 1 year, for which the Parent-Child Mother Goose Program is intended to run.

Despite difficulties recruiting participants, Jonathan was required to have adequate numbers of programs and participants to include with his annual reports to the foundation that sponsored the ASL Parent-Child Mother Goose Program. As a result, he regularly led programs with only hearing participants, who were the most robust and easily recruited group for the program. On the same dates when our 8-week program was held at DSA, Jonathan scheduled another program elsewhere in the city that included only hearing participants. Following each session of our program at DSA, Jonathan departed to lead a program in this alternate location. He reported that 10 families with hearing parents and children were registered for the alternate program. During interviews and observations, it emerged that for Jonathan, having two separate programs with distinct participant groups provided means for comparison between hearing and Deaf participants— for example, the kinds of rhymes they preferred, and the ease of running a program that included ASL-fluent Deaf mothers as compared to a program whose participants collectively lacked any experience with learning ASL.

These comparisons also served to highlight the mercenary nature of ASL instruction: In general, Canadian and American programs for teaching ASL have been directed at second-language learners, or hearing adults who pay for classes at service agencies and some postsecondary institutions, and teaching ASL as a second language is an employment opportunity and source of income for many Deaf individuals. (Many U.S. states have granted public high schools the right to assign foreign-language credit to ASL courses, and Deaf teachers are employed in some public schools for teaching ASL to mainly hearing students.) Baby sign programs for hearing parents and children are frequently taught by hearing instructors who run their classes as a business opportunity: For example, one Deaf mother participant told me that a popular baby sign program she attended, led by a hearing instructor, charges each registrant $140.

The phenomenon of Deaf adults teaching ASL as a first language to Deaf children (and as a second language to their parents) is more rare, outside of provincial or state schools for Deaf students that utilize a bilingual/bicultural approach; teaching ASL as a first language is also more poorly remunerated. According to an Ontario IHP agency policy and procedures manual, ASL and literacy consultants who provide ASL services to families under the IHP are paid $35 per hour, with a maximum of 1 hour per family per week for ASL instruction (a total of 48 hours of ASL instruction and 10 hours of consultation per year is allotted for each family requesting ASL services, until the child reaches the age of 6).

In contrast, Norwegian parents of Deaf and hard of hearing children are entitled to at least 40 weeks of free instruction in Norwegian Sign Language (NSL) and Deaf culture, including 900 hours of instruction in NSL during the child's first 16 years (Haualand & Hansen, 2007; Peterson, 2007). Swedish parents of Deaf children also receive signed language instruction in large, intensive blocks of time, including 3-day-weekend and

1- or 2-week courses (Mahshie, 1995). In a Canadian context, this shifting value of ASL as a resource, according to which group of persons is taught or teaches a version of the language, illustrates the aptness of Bourdieu's (1977) observation that I cited at the beginning of this chapter.

Public resources for Deaf children's learning of ASL are intrinsically tied to the presence of gatekeepers: professional individuals and institutions that regulate access to the language. My use of the term *gatekeeper* is borrowed from an open letter by Anita Small that was issued following an August 19, 2005, Provincial Court of Saskatchewan decision in the matter of the Child and Family Services Act and Ryley Allen Farnham. Ryley was an 8-year-old Deaf student with a cochlear implant who had been denied access to learning ASL by Saskatchewan health and education professionals and who possessed virtually no spoken, signed, or written language abilities. This letter concludes: "I implore all of us here who work with Deaf children and who are not Deaf ourselves, to be humble. . . . We as hearing individuals should not be the gatekeepers of the language. It is not ours to allow. It is theirs to have" (A. Small, October 25, 2007).

Like the matter of public resources for ASL, the impact of gatekeepers has been infrequently documented or held up to public scrutiny. For example, the operational policies of the Ontario IHP in regard to denying ASL services to children with cochlear implants have been largely unwritten (Snoddon, 2008). Policy set by Toronto's Hospital for Sick Children requires children who receive cochlear implants from this hospital to enroll in AVT and thereby reject ASL (V. Papaioannou, letter to the Ministry of Children and Youth Services, December 11, 2007); the Children's Hospital of Eastern Ontario in Ottawa has appeared to operate by a similar, but unwritten, policy. The cochlear implant program is housed with the AVT department in this same hospital (S. Weber, personal communication, April 25, 2008). The statements and conduct of individual medical and speech and hearing professionals in regard to the use of ASL by Deaf children and their families have been even less visible.

Gatekeeper Restrictions on Learning ASL and Perspectives on Deaf Identity

On the first afternoon of our program in a large, sunlit room at DSA, four participating mother/child dyads were in attendance— Alison and Tom, Bianca and Charlie, Donna and Violet, and Julia and Henry—as well as several observers. During Jonathan's opening presentation to the group of parents and children seated on a large foam mat, he introduced the ASL Parent-Child Mother Goose Program and explained some features of ASL, including the language's use of handshapes as phonological units and the roles of facial expression and mouth movements in conveying ASL grammar. He briefly outlined the history of DCO's ASL and literacy consultant and ASL Parent-Child Mother Goose programs, and the benefits to parents and children that are provided by the latter (including support for parent–child communication, interaction, and turn taking, and the development of different types of age-appropriate language skills in Deaf children). He described the structure and content of our 8-week program at DSA: Each session would begin with learning ASL rhymes and rhythms, then move to learning an ASL story, and end with a circle (a group rhyme or signing activity). Jonathan then demonstrated several different rhymes.

Two mothers with young children who had been observing our program from the back of the room joined in as the parents and children began learning and practicing the rhymes. The Deaf daughter of one of these two mothers had repeatedly wandered into the center of the mat where the participants were seated during Jonathan's demonstration. Jonathan assisted these mothers with learning the rhyme "Peekaboo Animals." After the session ended and registration forms were distributed, I asked the mother who had a Deaf daughter if she was interested in continuing to participate in the program. The mother explained that she first needed to obtain the permission of her child's AV therapist. This family did not attend any subsequent program sessions, although the mother and her child were glimpsed on the periphery of our program space when they again visited DSA.

Gatekeepers also hindered Jonathan's efforts to recruit more participants for our program. Two weeks after our program began, Jonathan and I attended a family event at DSA for parents and young children who were involved with the agency's programs. Jonathan shared information about the ASL Parent-Child Mother Goose Program at DSA with several hearing parents of young Deaf children. While doing so, Jonathan met Grace and David, and invited them to attend our program. However, another mother whom Jonathan approached stated that her child was going to receive a cochlear implant and that, following the hospital's advice, they would not be learning ASL. Jonathan attempted to give this mother various ASL and literacy information materials—brochures, booklets, and videotapes that had been developed by DCO—but she refused to accept them.

Research participants also reported gatekeeper prohibitions on and disapproval of learning ASL. Alison said that Tom's ear, nose, and throat physician (ENT) had expressed surprise that she and her son attended the program at DSA: "I think he doesn't understand why I'm learning ASL. He's like—just go and get your hearing aid and you'll be fine. That's good enough." In another conversation following our 6th program session, Alison commented on the negative language she experienced doctors and audiologists using in regard to hearing loss. Although one professional initially told her that Tom has normal hearing in one ear—his other ear has a severe hearing loss—another subsequently informed her that the first ear's hearing is "in the low range of normal—whatever that means."

The Deaf mother participants also commented on the attitudes and influence of gatekeepers. Following our program's second session, I observed a conversation between Donna and Julia about their experiences with the IHP. Donna said that Violet had been identified by the IHP as being at high risk for hearing loss because she carried a "bad gene." (Both Donna and her husband are Deaf, and her husband's family has a history of hereditary deafness. In my first interview with her, Donna had remarked on the phenomenon of Violet carrying a deafness gene.) As a consequence, hearing tests were ordered when Violet was born. Julia shared that an ENT had recently pressured her regarding a cochlear implant for Henry. She also commented that she sympathized with hearing parents who come under similar pressure from doctors and audiologists. Following our 6th program session, Julia said that an IHP representative had also approached her about a cochlear implant for Henry. She added that she felt that cochlear implants are promoted so heavily for financial reasons; it seemed to her that cochlear implant corporations want to eliminate the numbers of Deaf persons and also make a profit.

Bianca reported negative attitudes and prohibitions on ASL on the part of the speech and hearing professionals whom she encountered in seeking IHP services. During my first interview with her, Bianca explained that she and Charlie had started AVT but only attended one session. She also told me about her plans to start ASL and literacy consultant services. However, in subsequent interviews it became clear how much difficulty Bianca was having in gaining access to ASL services through the IHP; IHP staff members told her she did not qualify for ASL services because of Charlie's degree of hearing loss as it appeared in an audiogram. Bianca remarked to me that this position made no sense to her—what would happen if Charlie took off his hearing aids, or if he didn't like them?

In a later conversation, Bianca told me about her numerous referrals for hearing tests for Charlie and one referral to a cochlear implant surgeon in her city. (It is interesting to note that although Charlie's degree of hearing loss was deemed insufficient for him to receive ASL services, the same group of speech and hearing professionals who provided this opinion also referred him and his mother for consultation with a cochlear implant surgeon.) Bianca then said that she thought cochlear implants were only for profoundly Deaf children and that unlike with a hearing aid, with a cochlear implant "you can't go back." During the last program session Bianca provided more detail regarding her previous involvement with AVT—to which she was referred instead of the dual-language services that she had requested—and the censure she received from AVT professionals for expressing a desire to learn ASL:

> We're not taking AVT but auditory skills or auditory technology—but it seems to be the same thing, with a different name. Last September, I went to the first session and they said to me, "You understand this is auditory-verbal therapy?" I said "No, I thought this was auditory skills—because I also want sign language—ASL." That provoked a reaction from the speech-language pathologist: "Why are you doing that? Maybe he won't learn to speak." I said, "What I've read says you're wrong." So she started to argue with me. She asked me, "Do you speak with your son?" I said, "Yes, of course. I don't even know ASL yet. Only some basic words. So of course I speak. I only know the signs for words like mother, father, eat." The SLP said, "Well," and started to comment about that.

Due to gatekeeper influence, the extent and type of ASL and literacy resources that were available to Deaf and hearing mother participants differed.

Access to and Use of Resources

The Deaf and hearing mother participants in our program reported making different use of the same parent–child resources that were available to them. A main resource was a popular baby sign program designed for hearing parents and infants and led mainly by hearing instructors; Julia and Henry were involved as the only Deaf registrants. Julia described how she adapted its activities for use with Henry by adding more ASL vocabulary to the signs taught in class. For example, when one baby sign class taught some signs for food and eating, Julia added the ASL signs for CEREAL and GRAPES when communicating with Henry. During our 7th program session, when Jonathan advised the hearing mothers to take ASL classes, Julia suggested the baby sign program as a potential resource for these mothers, if they revised its content to better suit their children's needs.

Bianca had registered for, but not yet started attending, a different session of this baby sign program. During my first interview with her, she described the barriers to learning ASL that she and her husband faced. She was looking for ASL classes for her husband and herself, and although she knew that DSA offered ASL classes for adult students, she did not have child care for Charlie while she attended class. She learned most of the ASL vocabulary she knew from the *Sign With Your Baby* poster and book that she had at home. On several occasions, Bianca expressed her wish to learn more ASL through ASL services provided by the IHP. During my final interview with her, Bianca said, "I would absolutely love to have an ASL consultant. I would love, love, love one." I replied that I thought it was her right, and Bianca answered, "I think it should be."

Both Julia and Donna as Deaf mothers had participated with their children in mainstream early years programs and activities. During our 3rd session, Donna told the other participants about her involvement in weekly exercise classes for parents and infants. The other parents in these classes often sang together, and registrants received handouts with the lyrics for songs used in the program. Violet, as a hearing child, enjoyed listening to the parents singing. (Donna, as a Deaf mother, made additional references to the spoken-language and musical activities that she provided for Violet. In addition to attending the exercise class, Donna played music at home for Violet to listen to.) Julia also discussed her plans to join a mainstream aerobics program for mothers and toddlers when Henry reached 6 months of age.

However, both Deaf and hearing mother participants reported a lack of existing programs and resources geared toward ASL users. Following our program's 7th session, I asked Alison if she felt there was a need for more resources to support her own learning of ASL. Alison responded:

> It would be cool if we had a weekly class. Not just up to eight weeks. It would be really nice to have an ongoing program. Eight weeks isn't enough. What else is there? I can find a hearing Parent-Child Mother Goose Program, but I wish this one could continue.

Julia also said that she wished our program continued longer. She compared the length of our program to swimming lessons for parents and infants that normally run for 12 weeks. In an interview during our last session, I asked Julia about her plans to continue participating in ASL activities. She said that after our program ended, there wasn't much that was available to her and Henry aside from the rhymes that she used by herself at home, and the guidance provided by an ASL and literacy consultant. Donna also expressed regret at the end of our last ASL Parent-Child Mother Goose Program session: "Is the program really finished? The other mothers here want more—why can't we continue for two more weeks?"

In addition to a lack of existing resources, the parent participants reported a lack of awareness and information regarding programs and services appropriate for Deaf children and their families. I asked Grace, who left our program following its 7th session because her maternity leave had ended, if she had any plans to continue learning ASL. Grace expressed her uncertainty:

> For now, maybe we'll try to do what I've learned here. Then maybe later . . . because now I have to go back to work so I'll have a new schedule and new way of life, and I will put David in day care. So we'll have to get used to those new things. [I commented that Jonathan had plans to begin a new ASL Parent-Child Mother Goose Program at DSA in the new year but I was not sure whether Grace's schedule would permit her and David to attend.] Yes, it will be hard because I'm working. I work from 9 to 5.

Grace did not mention any potential difficulties for David in being placed in a mainstream day care setting. During this same interview, I asked Grace if she wished more ASL and early literacy resources were available to her as a parent. Because she appeared to hesitate, I asked if my question was clear. Grace responded: "Oh yes, you're clear. I understand—but I'm thinking. I don't know a lot about what's available. So if I knew, then maybe . . . but I don't know. I have to see what I can use. I don't know."

Although Mary told me in my first interview with her that she and Peter had moved to Canada in order for Sarah to receive a good education, they also faced a lack of existing services for Deaf children. (This family had started attending the alternate ASL Parent-Child Mother Goose Program that was held on the same day as our program at DSA, but switched to our program after learning that other Deaf parents and children would be present. In order to attend our program at DSA, Mary, Peter, and Sarah needed to take two different regional public transit systems. It was perhaps because of this onerous journey that the family only attended three sessions.) Peter told me about his experiences with regional IHP staff members and service providers. For example, the IHP family support worker for his region could not identify any day care services for Deaf children. This individual had informed Peter and Mary that Sarah could attend any day care center, but Peter had corrected her and asked about specialized day care services for Deaf children. Peter was aware of a day care program at a Deaf school outside his region, but he was told that the IHP would not assist with covering the costs of Sarah attending.

In addition to a lack of awareness on the part of IHP staff members, parent participants also reported a lack of advocacy. For example, rather than advocating for Bianca as a client, the family support worker for her region had suggested that Bianca write a letter to the IHP about her inability to gain access to ASL services for Charlie and herself. Bianca also mentioned difficulties with finding implements for Charlie's hearing aids and the cost of purchasing hearing aids. Before the start of our 6th program session, I observed Bianca talking with a DSA staff member about not being able to find a particular gadget for keeping Charlie's hearing aid attached to his shirt in order to prevent his hearing aid from being lost. After our session ended, Bianca complained that Charlie's hearing aids had cost $2,000 but only half of this cost was covered by the province's Assistive Devices Program. (At this time, I commented on the disparity of the province's health system funding all costs related to a cochlear implant.) The following week, in response to a question I asked about the gadget, Bianca also mentioned looking for a cover for Charlie's hearing aid to make it more comfortable for him to wear. Information about these implements did not appear to be readily available to her.

Costs and resources also appeared to preoccupy Jonathan. Only two families showed up for the program's 3rd session, and Jonathan commented, on this and other occasions, that if he charged parents for attending the program then they would be more inclined to attend. Jonathan also told me about his efforts, as an ASL and literacy consultant, to advocate for the families he taught; for example, for one family he had managed to secure an extension of the ASL services he provided. But none of the families of children with cochlear implants involved with his regional IHP agency had been referred to him for initial consultation or information about ASL services.

In a conversation following our 7th program session, Jonathan mentioned Ella Mae Lentz's ASL poem "The Treasure." In her poem, Lentz describes ASL as a glowing treasure that becomes buried beneath layers of oppression and disregard for the language. As Jonathan commented, many professionals involved with infant hearing screening and early intervention services for parents and Deaf children have no idea of the kinds of resources that the Deaf community offers. Jonathan compared the ASL

Parent-Child Mother Goose Program to the treasure in Lentz's poem.

Discussion

In his chronicle of the breakdown of community involvement in the formation of an Australian national language policy, Joseph Lo Bianco (2001) describes the dominance of "an overall discursive regime that has framed the worth of languages, their potential and meanings" using criteria that exclude users of minority languages "from converting their language knowledge into any other kind of capital" (p. 15). As Lo Bianco argues, if "intellectual, familial, local, cultural, or humanizing discourses were attached to languages," then any of these minority languages as mother tongues "would be allocated a multiple capital endowment" (p. 15). The framing of language and culture as commodities (Bourdieu, 1977) provides a lens for viewing the uneven distribution of resources by infant hearing screening and early intervention programs as described in this chapter. Efforts on the part of the Deaf community to convert its specialized knowledge and resources into practical initiatives for supporting ASL learning and bilingual education have met with resistance from government officials and public agencies, as evidenced by the lack of broad support for ASL services to families with Deaf children and for the ASL Parent-Child Mother Goose Program as a family ASL literacy program. Further, the Ontario IHP and its agents' contribution to language planning and policy for Deaf children, by restricting access to or failing to support the learning of ASL, has largely escaped scrutiny. Yet, as Lo Bianco also notes, a "commitment to provide equal access to educational opportunities" cannot be achieved in the case of Deaf or minority-language children "without systematic language policy and planning" (p. 25). Such a systematic language policy demands transparency and public accountability, a clear basis in empirical research, public employees who are able to offer appropriate guidance and support to parents of Deaf children, and adequate provisions for supporting early ASL acquisition.

The resistance to ASL that participants reported and that I observed in the course of coordinating arrangements for our program points to an institutionalized refusal to recognize the potential value of ASL for Deaf children and their families. One strand of this refusal is linked to the perspectives and attitudes of speech and hearing professionals regarding Deaf persons and signed language. In her anthropological study of an audiology clinic in the United States, Fjord (1999) describes the "stigma" of "being deaf in America" (p. 134) that endures in certain medical and academic quarters despite advances in Deaf studies and the popularity of ASL classes. As she writes, "When hearing parents take their child to 'see' a hearing specialist such as an otologist, ENT, or audiologist, along with the diagnosis in any society comes initiation into social meanings and ideologies about what it means to be a deaf person in this society" (Fjord, p. 126). In the discourse of American early intervention programs, "a Deaf identity and visual, signed language is a less-than-whole identity that must be 'fixed' no matter the financial or social cost" (Fjord, p. 124). Such social meanings and ideologies regarding Deaf people are neither universal nor unproblematic. Fjord analyzes the statements and conduct of American specialists in relation to their counterparts in Sweden and Denmark, where broader emphasis and support is placed on learning signed language and on modes of bilingual learning: "Deaf identity or personhood in Scandinavia is the performance not of a disability, but of a special status of linguistic minority group of visual people" (p. 127).

The encounters with gatekeepers and medical professionals described by Deaf and hearing mothers in this chapter, including the messages that Alison and Donna received about their children, support the view that Canadian health professionals have not offered a more positive vision of a Deaf identity than their American counterparts. In the discourse presented by Ontario speech and hearing professionals Tom's hearing is "in the low range of normal" and Violet carries a "bad gene" because of her Deaf parents. Julia's account of being pressured regarding a cochlear implant for Henry is in keeping with Ladd's (2003, 2007) account of British and American medical professionals attempting to force Deaf parents to have their Deaf children undergo cochlear implant surgery. Implicit in these statements and accounts are value judgments regarding the relative worth and position in Canadian society of Deaf people and their language and culture. The negative reactions of speech and hearing professionals toward Alison and Bianca's stated desire to learn ASL are in keeping with this discourse.

In Ladd's (2003) narration of the historical impact of colonialism on the Deaf community, the present-day medical model views "each born Deaf person" as "a helpless isolated hearing-impaired individual, with no intrinsic relationship with any other Deaf person, past or present, no group allegiances or history" (p. 163). Within this model, "these individuals can be 'restored to society' by the use of technology in conjunction with Oralism, especially if they are denied access to Deaf adults and sign languages" (Ladd, p. 163). In order to maintain itself, the medical discourse on Deaf persons necessarily opposes the phenomena of signed languages and Deaf culture, whether by denying the validity of the former or disputing the existence of the latter. If gatekeepers were to recognize the benefits of ASL and Deaf culture for all Deaf children, it would undercut the basis for their professions. However, Fjord's interviews with Swedish cochlear implant surgeons who speak of the need to ensure that Deaf children have access to signed language suggest that the medical discourse regarding Deaf people that Ladd describes may not always be natural, inevitable, or universal.

It remains an unsettling idea that some health and medical professionals in our midst—supported by public funds and working with public agencies—have acted in concert to disempower the

Deaf community and the contributions that its representatives might make toward enhanced language acquisition, parent–child interaction and communication, and education for Deaf children. Fjord emphasizes this incongruity in the actions of professionals whose work has the ostensible aim of caring for Deaf children when she describes the "usually immensely dedicated people, highly trained, and emotionally engaged in their work" (p. 125), whom she encountered in the persons of audiologists and otologists in an American lab. Fjord sees national cultural values behind the ethos of caring that underlies the conduct of speech and hearing professionals. Cultural values are also implicit in the kind of "magical thinking" that underlies the AVT prohibition on ASL and that sees "professionals in deafness . . . interacting with deaf people as if they weren't deaf, as if they didn't need visual contact to communicate" (Fjord, p. 126).

This kind of magical thinking seemingly underlies the Provincial Court of Saskatchewan decision regarding Ryley Farnham mentioned earlier in this chapter. In his decision, the presiding judge stated that "the evidence convinced me that the persons in authority who have dealt with Ryley [the Saskatchewan health and educational professionals] are people of great ability and great compassion" (Provincial Court of Saskatchewan, 2005, par. 5). The justice also described the "physicians and medical personnel, audiologists, educators, child protection workers, and others" who appeared before or who were described to the court as "undoubtedly caring and capable professionals" who had "acted in strict accordance with the policies, directives and mandates of the governmental or other bodies for whom they work" (Provincial Court of Saskatchewan, 2005, par. 5).

Some of the ASL Mother Goose families experienced similar treatment. Tom's ENT saw no reason for the child to learn ASL once his hearing aid was obtained, and Peter and Mary's IHP family support worker failed to comprehend Deaf children's need for specialized, accessible day care services. As outlined in chapter 2, young Deaf and hard of hearing children both need and significantly benefit from access to signed language. The failure of various professionals to recognize the role that ASL can play in these children's development speaks to entrenched problems in public systems purporting to serve Deaf children.

Fjord links the opposition to ASL in American culture to that country's traditional melting-pot stance on multiculturalism and push toward monolingualism: "the effort to shape an English-speaking, able-bodied, patriotic citizenry from a heteroglot immigrant population" (p. 123). In this culture, the attempted transformation from a Deaf to non-Deaf identity through cochlear implants and AVT is seen as "a 'miracle,' a 'cure'" (p. 126). Yet in Canada, public imagination often prides itself on an image of a tolerant, bilingual nation with a record of successful multiculturalism policies. In this context, public support for the language and culture of Deaf people as a part of and an intrinsic benefit to Canadian society seems appropriate and necessary.

However, under the auspices of a public health and early child care system, Ontario resources for young Deaf children have been largely allocated toward cochlear implant surgery and follow-up AVT habilitation instead of supports for bilingual learning. The same allocation of resources is true for many other provinces and countries. As Komesaroff (2007) writes, "The rate of childhood implantation in many countries is now estimated to involve 90 percent–95 percent of all children born deaf . . . The implementation of programs to screen the hearing of newborns . . . has resulted in children being identified and referred to implant clinics at a very young age" (pp. xi–xii). Bianca's report of receiving Ontario government support for only half the cost of Charlie's hearing aid, and little guidance for making this implement more comfortable for her son to wear, is apparently also typical of several other countries that have embraced childhood cochlear implant surgery. In the United States, Medicaid covers the entire cost of a cochlear implant but not of hearing aids; the same is true of private insurance (Fjord, 1999). However, the Hearing Loss Association of America (2009) now lists a number of states that have since passed legislation mandating some degree of health insurance coverage for children's hearing aids.

The lack of public support for learning ASL and the failure of public agencies to support existing ASL and early literacy resources provide the context for individual families' and the leader's participation in the ASL Parent-Child Mother Goose Program. These factors worked together to create both a Deaf cultural space for our program and a counterdiscourse to the medical view of Deaf individuals, their language, and their culture.

6 A Deaf Cultural Space

To ARGUE THAT our program environment and activities provided a Deaf cultural presence, it must be clear what Deaf culture is and how it was manifest in this setting. Carol Padden and Tom Humphries note that they have "used a definition of culture that focused on beliefs and practices, particularly the central role of sign language in the everyday lives of the community" (2005, p. 1). These authors make reference to the view of Deaf people as "seeing people" or "people of the eye," but add that "Deaf people's practices of 'seeing' are not necessarily natural or logical," as in terms of possessing "a heightened visual sense" (2005, p. 2). Rather, these "ways of 'seeing' follow from a long history of interacting with the world in certain ways—in cultural ways" (p. 2). Deaf schools, communities, employment, poetry, and theater, as well as signed languages, form part of this history. Padden and Humphries's focus on beliefs and practices reveals how an ASL and Deaf culture discourse is based on more than simply language. Like other discourses, Deaf culture involves, as well as particular uses of language, "distinctive ways of acting, interacting, valuing, feeling, dressing, thinking, believing, with other people and with various objects, tools, and technologies, so as to enact specific socially recognizable identities engaged in specific socially recognizable activities" (Gee, 2008, p. 155). A particular ASL discourse is tied to a particular social identity of being "culturally Deaf" and to particular settings and institutions like Deaf schools and Deaf clubs. Each discourse also invites its apprentices to play a particular role, but by participating in discourses individuals can also act to alter them in some way.

For instance, the increased participation of former mainstreamed Deaf students in present-day ASL and Deaf culture discourses has broadened the definitions of who counts as Deaf and who can play a role in these discourses.

We can glimpse these Deaf culture–based beliefs and practices, and this history of interacting with the world, in the theme of name signs in our program and in the distinct nature of the knowledge the Deaf participants in my study shared in regard to the features and uses of ASL and to ASL literacy practices. The unique features of this knowledge derive from its origins in a community of Deaf people for whom ASL is a first or primary language, who have grown up knowing the importance of visual communication for Deaf children, and whose professional experience has further developed this expertise with fostering early ASL literacy. This knowledge is largely absent from the discourse of Ontario speech and hearing and medical professionals as presented in this book, due in large part to the lack of resources for supporting ASL.

Several writers have chronicled the impact of 20th-century oralist discourses of mainstreaming and medical interventions, and of Deaf community counterdiscourses regarding Deaf people's ways of seeing (Ladd, 2003; Padden & Humphries, 2005). In particular, the recognition of signed language–using Deaf individuals as members of genuine linguistic communities and the advances in overall linguistic knowledge that have been gained by discoveries in signed language linguistics have greatly contributed to the recognition of Deaf culture and heritage. As Padden and Humphries note, "To possess a language that is not quite like other languages, yet equal to them, is a powerful realization for a group of people who have long felt their language disrespected and besieged by others' attempts to eliminate it" (2005, p. 157).

However, Ladd expresses the difficulties inherent in validating cultural recognition of the Deaf community, particularly in an academic domain in which Deaf people's experiences have been virtually excluded. As he argues, "Initially, in order to even establish the existence of a Deaf community, one has to work one's way through a series of ideological strata which attempt to deny its existence" (2003, p. 169). After overcoming these ideologies, researchers must contend with a dominant-culture view of the Deaf community "as a collection of individuals who are either less than normal or who have failed to achieve normality" (p. 169). Only after researchers "begin to attempt an honest academic description of a healthy Deaf community in its own terms" can the concept of Deaf culture be presented for consideration (pp.169–171). These difficulties are so pervasive because of the dominance of medical views of Deaf people as impaired, and because of mainstream, ethnocentric cultural values.

Ladd also discusses some ontological problems with defining the concept of culture and its application to communities of Deaf people. Just as definitions of "language" appeared to preclude signed languages prior to linguistic analyses of those languages, definitions of "culture" such as those provided by anthropology may need to be expanded to encompass Deaf culture, which is often not transmitted through the unit of the family. Additionally, there is a lack of clear boundaries to demarcate Deaf cultural groups, which include a diversity of experiences and a continuum of hearing loss—such as the presence of hard of hearing individuals who have been able to "pass" for much of their lives. As well, the facets of Deaf culture that mark it as a minority, colonized culture and as an entity habited by bilingual/bicultural actors who also participate in majority society render it distinct. Nonetheless, Ladd affirms the correspondence of Deaf communities to ethnicity distinctions (such as the high rate of endogamous marriage), linguistic criteria, and belief systems. A Deaf identity is also often consciously adopted by choice by former mainstreamed Deaf individuals.

The forces of mainstreaming and cochlear implants—with their concomitant discourse regarding isolating Deaf people from each other and denying access to native signed languages—have compelled Deaf communities to assert the validity of Deaf ways of being. These forces have been joined with developments in genetic engineering such as screening embryos for genes linked to deafness (see Emery, Middleton, & Turner, 2010), where efforts are aimed at eliminating the numbers of Deaf individuals. For Ladd, with these recent developments in genetics it becomes necessary to define Deaf people's contribution to the human race as a condition of their survival. As he argues, "Features of Deaf people's positive biology include enhanced visual skills; sensitivity to touch and enhanced general tactility; and enhanced use of face, hands, and bodies. Indeed, Deaf languages have emerged from precisely this foundation" (2007, p. 2). These positive features "have led to a remarkably high degree of globalism among Deaf people; the syntactic similarities and profound 'plasticity' of their languages" suggest that signing Deaf communities "set a contrasting example to the (hearing) human history of war and oppression" (2007, p. 2)—the contrast owing to the relative ease with which Deaf signers from different countries are able to communicate and share affinity with each other as compared to hearing users of different spoken languages.

With its incorporation of Deaf adults' visual, tactile, and interactive uses of language with young children, the ASL Parent-Child Mother Goose Program functions both to support and demonstrate Deaf people's positive biology. In these terms, the program itself can be said to present a counterdiscourse to not only pathologic views of Deaf individuals, but also the national cultural values that entwine with this medical discourse. With such a discourse unmasked and its embodiment in infant hearing screening and early intervention services brought to light, increased support for the alternate views and initiatives of the Deaf community of ASL users becomes a matter of human rights.

Padden and Humphries also note that Deaf researchers of Deaf culture must examine their personal histories in light of their analyses. As these authors write, "We understand now that our personal lives are intertwined in the very same history we describe . . . and that we too are implicated in 'the promise of culture'" (2005, p. 8). It is for much the same reason that I make reference to my own experiences and situatedness at various points in this book.

Names and Naming in a Family ASL Literacy Program

The fact that a majority of adult—as well as child—participants in our program were Deaf meant that our program became a Deaf cultural space in a way that may not have happened had my participant group been constituted as I first envisioned it, with only hearing parents and Deaf children. Having both Deaf and hearing parent participants also allowed me to compare their perspectives on the social construction of Deaf identity. One factor that illuminated the presence of a Deaf cultural space, illustrated part of Jonathan's role and goals as a program leader, and led to discussions of Deaf culture among participants was the function of name signs.

During our first program session at DSA, after Jonathan had introduced me to the other participants and I briefly described my study and role as a researcher, I asked if the parents and children who were present could introduce themselves. Donna was the first parent participant to respond. When doing so, she used her own name sign and also signed Violet's name instead of fingerspelling its spoken-language counterpart. Donna added that Violet was 6 months old and is hearing, whereas Donna herself is Deaf.

After I introduced our interpreter and her name sign, Bianca was the next mother to respond. Using spoken English, she told us that Charlie was 8 months old. Bianca added that she herself is hearing and Charlie is hard of hearing.

The next mother, Julia, stood and rocked Henry in her arms as she introduced herself and her son in ASL. Like Donna, Julia used Henry's name sign when introducing him to the group. She added that Henry is Deaf and would be 5 months old in a week. Julia then turned so the group on the mat could view Henry's sleeping face as it rested against her shoulder.

Alison introduced herself in English and told us that Thomas was 5 ½ months old and that his left ear is Deaf and his right ear is hearing.

When Grace and David arrived partway through our 3rd program session, the Deaf and hearing mothers introduced themselves to her with the same use of ASL and spoken English names. I introduced her to Jonathan and the other parents by fingerspelling her name. Grace told us that David was 10 months old.

Peter, Mary, and Sarah also arrived near the end of the 3rd session. Peter and Mary, whose first language is LSM, used their own name signs and the name sign of their daughter, each of which employed a hand configuration that is not found in ASL. Mary also announced that Sarah would soon be 12 months old.

Unlike the children of Deaf parents, the children with hearing mothers did not have name signs at the start of our program. Name signs and the rules governing their assignment and use proved to be a significant theme. Although names and naming are frequently taken for granted, in each culture they are essential for socialization into a group of people (Supalla, 1992). Deaf members of the ASL community have two sets of proper names, one in ASL and another in English. Historically, name signs were given almost exclusively to Deaf people, and they mark an individual's membership in the Deaf community (Supalla). Name signs are assigned to individuals by another Deaf person, whether an authority figure of some kind, a Deaf parent or parents, or a peer group member at a Deaf school (Supalla). Other researchers have reported that name signs have been most commonly assigned by Deaf student peers (perhaps due to the fact that most Deaf children do not have Deaf parents and have traditionally acquired ASL and Deaf culture after arrival at a Deaf residential school; Meadow, 1977; Mindess, 1990).

Use of ASL Names

We first discussed name signs when the Deaf mothers in our program shared information about their interactions and use of language play with their children. Near the end of our 2nd session, Donna mentioned a simple ASL rhyme that she used with Violet. When greeting her daughter, Donna was in the habit of rhythmically signing HELLO, VIOLET three times using Violet's name sign, and then signing BYE-BYE, VIOLET in the same way when she left her daughter. At this time, Julia added that she often signed GOOD NIGHT, HENRY or GOOD MORNING, HENRY to her son when he was seated in his high chair.

During this conversation Jonathan commented that unlike how spoken English names are used, Deaf people do not use name signs when signing hello or goodbye to each other. ASL names are customarily used only to refer to a third person who is not present, and not when greeting someone or trying to get his or her attention (Supalla, 1992). Jonathan then demonstrated attention-getting behaviors used by Deaf people, such as waving an outstretched hand and making eye contact. As he remarked, a signer will first establish visual attention with another person, rather than call them by name, and then start a dialogue. Jonathan added that hearing individuals would usually not have name signs, and fingerspelled English names could not be used in a rhyme like the one Donna had improvised.

Jonathan then referred to ASL rhymes that involve a child's name sign. It appeared that like the language play the Deaf mothers improvised, ASL rhymes for young children present an exception to the customary use of ASL names for only a third person who is not present. Jonathan mentioned the rhyme "Where's Lisa?" that uses a child's name sign. Jonathan also demonstrated the rhyme "Mommy and Daddy Love You" using the same name sign:

MOMMY LOVES LISA,
DADDY LOVES LISA.
MOMMY AND DADDY LOVE LISA.
WHO'S LISA? WHO? (Jonathan here demonstrated the use of non-manual features to show he was asking a question.)
LOOK, IT'S YOU! (The adult signer or signers point at the child whose name sign is featured in the rhyme.)[1]

Jonathan remarked that he would use an ASL name in this rhyme, but never when addressing another individual in normal conversation. (As in the "Where's Lisa?" rhyme, "Mommy and Daddy Love You" involves the adult signer pretending to search for a child whose name sign is used in the third person.) Jonathan also stated that the use of names may be different for hearing babies and that we could compare how Deaf and hearing people use names. He emphasized for our group how name signs are an integral part of Deaf culture.

At this point in the conversation, Alison asked how name signs worked. Jonathan replied that the Deaf community assigns name signs. He explained that he received his own name sign at what was then the Ontario School for the Deaf (OSD), Belleville, when he was a young child, and asked the other Deaf adults how they received their name signs. They also described receiving their name signs in a Deaf school setting. Jonathan added that hearing people cannot give each other name signs—they should finger-spell each other's names instead; socializing with the Deaf community will lead to the giving of name signs. Donna interjected

---

1. To convey a sense of the ASL rhymes and stories used in our program, I have provided an English translation for several examples. However, these translations are not intended to be official or verbatim transcriptions or glosses. I also do not always follow ASL word order—which is often distinct from English—in my translations.

that Deaf parents can also give name signs to their children and then remarked to Alison, "Oh right, you are hearing." She told Alison that the other participants would observe Thomas during the program each week and figure out what his name sign would be.

Issues Surrounding Name Sign Formation

The following week, when seated on the mat and interacting with Thomas before the start of our program session, I had another conversation with Donna about name signs. At the time, I was trying to suggest some possible name signs for Tom by signing a T handshape on my right temple and a T handshape on my left front shoulder. However, Donna told me that we needed to observe more of Tom's characteristics and personality before giving him a name sign. (Although this was not mentioned, there may also have been some reservations regarding my qualifications to assign name signs as a nonnative ASL user.) Donna mentioned Violet's name sign and the name sign of another Deaf acquaintance: both individuals have nonarbitrary, or descriptive name signs that do not involve fingerspelled letters.

At this point, Donna mentioned Supalla's *Book of Name Signs* (1992) and asked me if I had read it. She explained that she preferred to avoid using fingerspelled letters in name signs because it means the name signs are borrowing from English. I remarked on Supalla's discussion of arbitrary name signs. These name signs, with no meaning other than their representation of the first fingerspelled letter of an individual's spoken-language first and/or last name, are traditional among Deaf ASL users. Arbitrary name signs are also described as "the native name sign system due to its preference and use among Deaf parents" (p. 17). Elsewhere, Supalla comments that Deaf parents "universally choose" the arbitrary name sign system over the descriptive name sign system to name their children (Supalla, 1990, p. 122). He argues that if all Deaf children had Deaf parents, the arbitrary name sign system would be the "primary name sign system" in the Deaf community (Supalla, 1990, p. 122). Using his own name sign as an example, Supalla (1990) offers a trenchant linguistic defense of arbitrary name signs' independence from English and conformity to ASL phonological parameters. Arbitrary name signs with some distinctive features are also the predominant name sign category among users of Classic Ontario ASL, the dialect of ASL formerly used by students of OSD (Hemingway, 2007).

Donna disagreed with the use of arbitrary name signs. She indicated a preference for descriptive name signs, the second ASL name system described by Hemingway (2007) and Supalla (1990, 1992). These name signs are based on some personal characteristic of the individual instead of on the first fingerspelled letter of a spoken/written name, and follow ASL linguistic rules: Instead of fingerspelled letters, these name signs employ handshape classifiers for referring to a physical characteristic (Supalla, 1990, 1992). The ASL community has historically considered descriptive name signs to be more childish. Indeed, Deaf children most frequently bestow and received this type of name sign (Padden, 1992); for example, peers bestow name signs to Deaf children of hearing parents at Deaf residential schools (Supalla, 1990). But Donna saw this type of name sign as superior to arbitrary name signs. A preference for descriptive name signs may also be more prevalent among younger generations of ASL users, particularly those with some international experience. Living or working with the Deaf community in other countries where native signed languages do not follow ASL arbitrary name sign conventions can lead to the assigning of new, descriptive name signs based on the naming conventions of another signed language. However, more research is needed to explore the evolution of ASL community members' attitudes toward both arbitrary and descriptive name signs.

The above conversations with Jonathan and Donna highlight a sociolinguistic tension surrounding some traditional aspects and uses of ASL in light of more recent efforts by the Deaf community and bilingual/bicultural educators to unpack the effects left by decades of monolingual, oralist education, as well as by the spread of ASL as a commodity among hearing learners. Notably, nontraditional name signs that violate ASL linguistic conventions have proliferated: These name signs have emerged at least in part due to the popularity of classes for hearing students learning ASL as a second language (Supalla, 1992). Nontraditional name signs tend to combine features of both descriptive and arbitrary name signs by employing both the first letter of an individual's name in addition to referring to some personal characteristic. In so doing, these name signs violate linguistic rules for the formation of both arbitrary and descriptive name signs. According to Supalla, Deaf ASL teachers have frequently given nontraditional name signs to their hearing students. The author suggests that this phenomenon may be a result of ASL instructors attempting to accommodate their student's misconceptions about name signs, such as their always having an inherent meaning. In addition, nontraditional name signs may be bestowed to mark the individual's identity as an ASL learner or a hearing person who is not an integral part of the Deaf community. Nontraditional name signs can therefore simultaneously represent sites of submission and resistance by the Deaf community: submission to the wishes and values of hearing outsiders, and resistance to these outsiders' encroachment on Deaf cultural markers.

However, researchers have also observed that many mainstreamed Deaf students are ignorant of the linguistic rules and cultural conventions behind name signs; these students have often come up with nontraditional name signs for each other (Mindess, 1990). Supalla calls it "a serious misconception that name signs are strictly descriptive in nature" and states this is evidence that there is "virtually no knowledge of the arbitrary name sign system" (1990, p. 100) among a segment of the ASL community. The use of nontraditional name signs by mainstreamed Deaf students also illustrates how an ASL discourse is acquired and adapted by individuals arriving "late in the game" (Gee, 2008, p. 179). In their performance of being or becoming a "real" Deaf user of ASL, previously mainstreamed Deaf students who bear nontraditional name signs can unwittingly set themselves apart from native ASL users and residential school students. However, as Gee notes, "There are no all-at-once, once-and-for-all, tests for who is adept" at being a particular social identity, because such phenomena as traditional and nontraditional name signs "emerge over the course of a developing history among groups of people" (pp. 160–161). A judgment of Deaf identity based on an individual's name sign "is embedded within situations that . . . make such judgments intrinsically provisional" (p. 161).

The growth of nontraditional name signs among Deaf ASL users may be accommodated in one or more ways. Some previously mainstreamed Deaf students can have their nontraditional name signs modified by native ASL users to make these name signs better conform to ASL naming conventions and linguistic structures, as happened with my own name sign. (The original twisting motion on my cheek of the middle fingertip of a K handshape was modified by one user of Classic Ontario ASL to become a firm tapping motion of the same fingertip. I was told this name sign was a permissible formation in Classic Ontario ASL, although it does not appear in Supalla's *Book of Name Signs*). Or certain formations of nontraditional name signs (such as name signs for women that employ a fingerspelled letter and mark the characteristic of having long hair) may have become so widespread that they are (usually) accepted without comment by the Deaf community. Or, while recognizing formerly mainstreamed Deaf students as part of the Deaf community, some Deaf people can continue to express hope that some day, more Deaf students will have the benefit of ASL and Deaf Studies programs and curricula from an early age so that a historic ASL discourse is rendered "visible, valuable, and meaningful" (Gee, p. 188) by schools and early intervention programs. Through exposure to this ASL

discourse, linguistic rules and historic conventions for the formation of name signs may be better understood and valued.

Donna's comments about her preference for nonarbitrary name
signs also highlighted a resistance to the perceived influence of
English on some aspects of ASL. As an example, Donna cited the
name sign of Laurent Clerc, who was the first Deaf teacher at
the American School for the Deaf in Hartford, Connecticut, the
nation's first permanent school for Deaf students. Clerc's name
sign employs the H handshape but does not derive from Clerc's
English (or French) name. However, Clerc's descriptive name
sign originates in Langue des signes française (LSF) and does not
follow ASL name sign conventions (Supalla, 1992). In any case,
Clerc brought what became ASL's fingerspelled alphabet—in addition to LSF—with him when he arrived in the United States
in 1816 (Supalla, 1992), which is when the arbitrary name sign
system is argued to have originated there. Evidence exists of the
use of arbitrary name signs among students at American Deaf
schools from as early as the 1820s (Supalla, 1992).

Giving of Name Signs

As it turned out, in the course of our program, most of the children of hearing parents received what appeared to be arbitrary
name signs. During our 5th program session, Jonathan again introduced "Mommy and Daddy Love You." He began by signing
the rhyme with Violet, but stopped when he realized that the
rhyme needs name signs. Turning to Julia, Jonathan confirmed
Henry's name sign, and then looked at Bianca, who did not have
a name sign for Charlie. At this point, Jonathan told Bianca to
wait until Charlie received his ASL identity sign at a Deaf school.
Jonathan then resumed demonstrating the rhyme with Violet's
name sign. When he finished, he commented that use of this particular rhyme encourages children to identify their own names.

Moments later, however, as Jonathan watched me attempting
to sign "Mommy and Daddy Love You" with David while finger-

spelling David's name, he announced that he would give David a name sign. This was an arbitrary name sign that appears in Supalla's *Book of Name Signs* and that employs the first letter of David's name. Jonathan then waved to David in order to get his attention. Seated in his mother's lap, David looked away from Jonathan, who clapped his hands in a 1, 2; 1, 2, 3 rhythm. Jonathan continued to clap until David looked at him with a smile. Jonathan stood and signed "Mommy and Daddy Love You" to David, using David's new name sign. Grace smiled in response, and Jonathan told her to try signing the rhyme herself. As Grace (who did not know any ASL before enrolling in our program) asked Jonathan to again show her the different signs used in the rhyme, he demonstrated David's name sign for her and then checked with the other Deaf adults in the room to see if they liked it. Both Donna and Julia agreed on the fitness of David's name sign and tried signing it themselves. Jonathan told Grace that she should tell David his name sign again and again. He showed her how to sign the sentence YOUR NAME SIGN IS DAVID. Grace shyly tried signing this sentence.

At this point, I tapped Jonathan's shoulder for attention and told him that he had forgotten Charlie. Jonathan turned to see Charlie sitting in front of Bianca and instantly created a name sign for him. Charlie's name sign appeared to be a nontraditional name sign, as it combined features of arbitrary and descriptive name signs; it was based on his tendency to laugh, as well as on the first letter of his English name. Bianca tried signing Charlie's name, and Jonathan taught her the same sentence that he had shown Grace, YOUR NAME SIGN IS CHARLIE. Jonathan then announced Charlie's name sign to the other participants. The adults practiced signing Charlie's name. Next Jonathan surveyed the group of children on the mat and signed their names: Sarah, Charlie, Violet, Henry, and David. Everyone had a name sign.

As Jonathan remarked when Tom received his own name sign 1 week later, a child's ASL identity or name sign may change when he or she goes to school. Here, Mary announced her plans to change Sarah's name sign when she was slightly older. There are many other children with name signs like Sarah's, and Mary felt this could become confusing. However, Alison stated that Tom wouldn't attend a Deaf school because he has a lot of hearing. A substantial discussion ensued regarding a name sign for Tom. Jonathan asked Alison what she had observed of Tom's personality and character. Alison responded that Tom tended to be quiet and calm. She also remarked that Tom was born during a full moon. The name sign that Jonathan gave to Tom appeared to be an arbitrary name sign, although its particular formation is not featured in the *Book of Name Signs'* list of arbitrary name signs following each alphabetic handshape. Some Classic Ontario ASL name signs appear to be distinct to this dialect, and it is possible that Tom's name sign is correct for Ontario users of ASL. However, Jonathan's emphasis on a name sign that reflected Tom's personality and characteristics may be indicative of the complex formation of name signs and of what was for Jonathan a tension surrounding the assigning of name signs in a nontraditional setting.

Researchers have observed that Deaf individuals prefer to wait until they are somewhat familiar with a recipient before granting his or her name sign (Mindess, 1990), and that even arbitrary name signs need to "'feel right'" (Mindess, p. 13) for the namer to give to the recipient. Some Classic Ontario ASL users have mentioned the existence of certain connotations behind their arbitrary name signs. In Classic Ontario ASL, the category of arbitrary name signs is subdivided into relative arbitrary name signs (following an individual's written first or last name), nonrelative arbitrary name signs (following an alphabetical handshape that is unrelated to the individual's written name), or unique arbitrary name signs (following an ASL handshape that is not included in the fingerspelled alphabet; Hemingway, 2007). There is mention of narratives about name signs by Classic Ontario ASL users, including some descriptions of unique arbitrary name signs that involved a particular handshape being used for all members of a certain group of students at OSD (Snoddon, 2010). However, these connotations behind arbitrary name signs often appear to be tenuous and group-oriented, in comparison to the explicit, individualistic significance of nontraditional name signs. Although Jonathan observed many of the traditional conventions behind name signs, it is unclear whether he consciously attempted to follow all of the linguistic rules for forming arbitrary and descriptive name signs for the children in our program.

It is also possible that Jonathan gave some child participants in our program what appear to be nontraditional name signs because he intended for these ASL identity markers to be used temporarily, until the participants were given name signs in settings that better recognized the individual children's contributions toward and presence in the Deaf community. This possibility is strengthened by Jonathan's initial reluctance to bestow name signs on the children of hearing parents and by his repeated references to receiving a name sign at a Deaf school. In fact, deaf people have several opportunities throughout their lives when they can enter the Deaf community, and the "assignment of a name sign can be seen as a kind of *rite de passage,* defining this entrance to the community" (Meadow, 1977, p. 239).

The theme of name signs in our program raises the question of whether infant hearing screening and early intervention services—insofar as they include provisions for learning ASL—might come to fundamentally alter the circumstances under which many Deaf children first encounter the Deaf community and thereby receive their name signs. The functions and descriptions of name signs in our program may also reflect the ways in which ASL names differ from names in a written or spoken language and reflect the role of the individual in Deaf culture. In a Deaf cultural space, the individual may often be defined in terms of his or her contributions toward and participation in the group.

Rather than a name sign being a token automatically bestowed on any Deaf person, it is a mark of his or her "personal efforts . . . and personal characteristics" (Delpit, 1988, p. 289), displayed for the ASL community to assess and embrace.

The issue of name signs for the children of hearing parents in our program was initially a source of concern for me. As a Deaf person who grew up outside of the Deaf community, I was concerned about the children of hearing parents being recognized and accepted by the Deaf adults and children in our program. For me, the assigning of name signs represented these children's inclusion in the Deaf community. I initially felt that waiting for a Deaf child to receive his or her name sign at school, as Jonathan suggested, was counterproductive to the goal of ensuring early ASL acquisition for Deaf children and hearing parents. I saw our program at DSA as an opportunity for hearing parents and Deaf children to become familiar with the Deaf community at an early stage in the children's lives, and name signs were a mark of having made this acquaintance. As Meadow (1977) writes, only Deaf children of Deaf parents have traditionally received their name signs in infancy, although not all such children receive their name signs at this stage of life or from their parents (Supalla, 1990).

In this regard, watching John Hemingway's *Classic Ontario ASL: Name Signs* DVD was instructive. The DVD's featuring of Deaf Ontarians—some in their 80s and 90s—reciting the name signs of former classmates from old photographs and school enrollment records gave me a better sense of the unique history, weight, and significance of name signs and their granting by the Deaf community. This matter also served to remind me of Lisa Delpit's advice to "believe that people are rational beings, and therefore always act rationally. We may not understand their rationales, but that in no way militates against the existence of these rationales or reduces our responsibility to attempt to apprehend them" (1988, p. 297). As Delpit adds, becoming "ethnographers in the true sense" means "we must learn to be vulnerable enough to allow our world to turn upside down in order to allow the realities of others to edge themselves into our consciousness" (p. 297). Having grown up in mainstream schools, there are some aspects of Deaf culture and history, and of an ASL discourse, of which I will never have a first-hand grasp. As I came to learn, not only did Jonathan authentically represent these Deaf historical traditions in his teaching of the program, but also his actions and comments were always guided by a strong commitment to and regard for the knowledge and values of Deaf people.

7   Facilitating Emergent ASL Literacy

IN THE DEAF cultural space of our program, the role and contributions of Deaf and hearing parents became central issues. In addition to my observations of the program, several conversations and interviews with Jonathan allowed me to further study his role and goals as a program leader. Against this backdrop of Deaf and hearing adult participant roles, the responses of individual children to the rhymes and stories used in our program became an additional focus.

Deaf Mothers as ASL and Literacy Experts

From the first, the Deaf mothers in our program were presented as experts in ASL and its use to foster language and literacy in young children. During our 1st program session, Jonathan introduced Donna and Julia to the other mothers as trained ASL Parent-Child Mother Goose Program leaders. In the course of our program, Jonathan also frequently discussed practice with the Deaf mothers in terms of developing and teaching ASL rhymes. The Deaf mothers provided an invaluable resource for supporting the other participants' learning about emergent ASL literacy.

Deaf Mothers' Use of ASL Rhymes and Home ASL Literacy Practices: Improvisations to ASL Rhymes and Creation of New Rhymes

A central issue for the use of ASL literature with young children in our program was the creation of additions and revisions to existing ASL rhymes. This issue highlighted what may be a unique feature of supporting emergent ASL literacy in young children:

the need to foster and sustain visual attention in order to support communication and language development. In order to attract and retain young children's visual attention, the Deaf mothers and Jonathan continually improvised new variations for existing rhymes that changed the original rhymes' tempo and increased their tactile and interactive components.

In an interview following our 7th session, Julia noted that she always signed certain rhymes in the same way, but with others she frequently made revisions and added detail. She stated that making these revisions encouraged Henry to be more attentive and provided more opportunities for his language development. For example, during the program's 2nd session Julia devised a variation of "ILY Balloon." This rhyme involves the adult signer pretending to blow on his or her thumb—as in blowing up a balloon—as the fingers of his or her dominant hand rise into the combined LY handshape.[1] Although this handshape is a phono-logical unit of several different signs, it is also used for one way of signing "I love you" in ASL. The signer then pretends to tie the ends of the ILY balloon, which descends toward the child. In this episode, not only did Julia initiate the use of a rhyme that Jonathan had not yet introduced—as she also occasionally did during later program sessions—but she also demonstrated several variations of this rhyme. She alternately signed the bal-loon descending rapidly—as if losing air—toward Henry, and gradually floating downward. In response, Henry lifted his arms as if to try and catch the balloon and clamped down with his mouth on Julia's index finger as the combined LY handshape landed on his chest. He then smiled and kicked his legs. As Julia concluded each variation of "ILY Balloon," she repeatedly asked Henry, MORE? AGAIN? to foster and sustain communication with

---

1. For right-handed signers, the right hand is the dominant hand in two-handed signs where each hand has a different handshape, while the left hand is the base hand. The reverse is true for left-handed signers (Valli & Lucas, 1995).

her son. As Julia continued to sign this rhyme, Alison watched her attentively and then practiced signing the rhyme with Tom, who like Henry lay in front of his mother on the mat.

During this episode, Julia also improvised a different rhyme, which she called "Balloon Numbers," that was based on "ILY Balloon." In this rhyme, Julia blew up the fingers of her dominant hand one by one into a 5 handshape. As she continued signing "Balloon Numbers," she alternated blowing up her fingers from her index finger to her pinky, and from her pinky to her index finger.[2] Henry lay still and watched his mother intently as she signed, then began kicking his legs rhythmically and waving his arms as the 5 handshape balloon started to descend toward him. AGAIN? Julia asked. Again she signed the rhyme, blowing up her fingers from pinky to index finger with emphatic movements. The 5 handshape balloon then dropped abruptly onto the mat beside Henry, who blinked. Julia blew up her fingers again and the 5 handshape descended in a fluttering motion, like a leaf falling from a tree onto Henry's face. He clutched his mother's hand in his fists as it descended. Jonathan called the other mothers' attention toward Julia's several improvisations.

Increase of Rhymes' Tactile Components

Both Donna and Julia suggested improvisations that increased the tactile and interactive components of rhymes and thus enhanced their suitability for very young children. As Donna explained, very young children like her daughter enjoyed rhymes that involved touch. She noted that Violet would enjoy rhymes that required more receptive skills when she was slightly older. Julia described how she had made adaptations to "Jolly Bear,"

---

2. Despite its title, Anita Small has noted that this rhyme may be more properly viewed as an instance of nonlinguistic play, or finger play, since the sequence devised by Julia does not produce all ASL numbers 1–5 and not all of the digits produced in this sequence correspond to ASL numbers.

a rhyme that Jonathan demonstrated during the 1st session. The original version of "Jolly Bear" is as follows:

> BEAR, BIG EARS on adult signer.
> BIG EARS on baby.
> BEAR, PUFFY CHEEKS on adult signer.
> PUFFY CHEEKS on baby.
> BEAR, BEAR on adult signer.
> BEAR on baby.
> BEAR, JOLLY TUMMY on adult signer.
> JOLLY TUMMY on baby.

In this rhyme, the adult signer's descriptions of the bear's physical features involve spread C handshapes—which are similar to the clawed 5 handshapes used in the ASL word BEAR—moving from the crown of the head to the cheeks to the shoulders to the sides of the lower torso (see figure 1). Following her mention of adaptations to this rhyme, Julia demonstrated a revised version of this rhyme in which she signed BEAR on Henry following each instance when she signed the word on herself, in addition to signing the bear's ears, cheeks, shoulders, and tummy on Henry. Julia remarked that Henry was learning about himself and his mother when she signed first on her own body and then his.

Donna also increased the tactile component of "Spider Roll Up and Down," an ASL adaptation of "Inky Winky Spider." Jonathan first demonstrated the rhyme with the doll he often used during the program:

> The sun shines down on baby, its rays beating with a 1, 2, 3 rhythm. Spider, rolled up into a ball, starts poking its legs out and upwards, one by one. Five legs turn over and begin crawling on baby. Clouds appear and rain starts to fall with a 1, 2, 3 rhythm. One by one, Spider's legs curl up and disappear into a ball that rolls rapidly down and away from baby. The sun reappears and starts beating down again with a 1, 2, 3 rhythm. Spider's legs emerge one by one, turn over, begin crawling over baby's torso, and tickle baby.

In this rhyme, a contracted 5 handshape is used for the sun's rays beating, a S handshape for the spider's body rolled into a ball,

FIGURE 1. "Jolly Bear." From *The ASL Parent-Child Mother Goose Program: American Sign Language Rhymes, Rhythms and Stories for Parents and Their Children* [DVD]. Copyright 2004 by the Ontario Cultural Society of the Deaf. Used with permission.

and crooked 5 handshapes for the rain falling. When signing this rhyme with her daughter, Donna made emphatic use of touch. She signed a spider unfurling and crawling directly onto a wriggling Violet, and used her base hand that became the unfurled spider to hold her daughter's leg still while she signed clouds and then rain. In doing so, Donna kept Violet's visual attention trained on her throughout the rhyme.

Similarly, when the participants signed "Elephant Looking for a Friend," Donna advised that the adult signer could make additional use of his or her trunk to wave at and pat the child for attention. This rhyme uses an extended B handshape for the elephant's trunk, the extended C handshape for SEARCH, and the crooked 1 handshape for FRIEND:

Elephant with her trunk waving begins searching left and right.
Searching, searching for a friend.
Elephant with her trunk waving searches left and right.
Searching, searching for a friend.
Elephant searches and searches for a friend.
Elephant sees one! Her trunk pats baby.
Found! Elephant's trunk pats baby happily.

Julia reported that she was most able to keep Henry's attention when she signed rhymes that involved her standing and stomping on the floor. He liked the vibrations and movement.

Creation of ASL Literacy and Numeracy Activities

The Deaf mothers created rhymes that fostered emergent literacy and numeracy by incorporating the concepts of counting and numbers. During our final program session, Donna demonstrated for the other participants how she signed numbers 1 to 5 with Violet. As Violet lay on the mat in front of her mother, Donna began signing the numbers 1, 2, 3, 4, 5 to Violet, who babbled with her hands in response. Donna's 5 handshape then fluttered down like a snowflake onto Violet's face. Violet blinked. Donna explained to the other participants that they could sign numbers 1 to 5 with both hands. First one hand and then the other can alternate signing numbers, then become a snowflake falling down. Then the signer can hold up both 5 handshapes and twist his or her wrists, as in the sign for FINISH. Jonathan praised Donna's innovation and asked her to sign the rhyme again.

Here Donna also demonstrated various tactics for keeping a child's visual attention trained on an adult signer. As Violet waved and then held her fists to her mouth, Donna touched her daughter's arms and then began clapping. With her nondominant or base hand, Donna signed numbers 1, 2, 3, 4, 5 to Violet, who watched and blinked as the 5 handshape became a snowflake fluttering down. Violet then held out her own hand in a 5 handshape, and laughed as her mother's fingertips brushed her face. With her dominant hand, Donna again signed numbers 1, 2, 3,

4, 5. Violet watched, closed her eyes, and smiled as the 5 hand-shape fluttered down to her face. Donna brushed Violet's face with both of her hands as she finished the rhyme. She explained to Jonathan and the other participants that the numbers 6, 7, 8, 9, and 10 can be added later on. Julia then asked Donna if the 5 handshapes fluttering down could also signify rain or leaves falling. Julia suggested different ways for signing a descending 5 handshape.

During our 7th program session, Julia shared further information about her home ASL literacy practices when she reported that Henry enjoyed learning his fingerspelled and printed letters and numbers. She had placed a mirror for Henry in his room at home that had peel-off stickers of numbers and letters. Julia described how she lifted Henry up in front of the mirror and bounced him in rhythm as she signed and pointed to the letters. The rhythm she used was similar to that of the alphabet song, "Now I know my ABCs," a song for hearing children that Julia adapted in order to teach Henry both fingerspelled and printed letters. She described how he laughed in response to her signing letters and then grabbed at the letter stickers. Julia also explained how she signed numbers 0 to 10 in front of the mirror and then asked Henry, "Where's 10?" with a befuddled expression. She would then move the stickers with the numbers 1 and 0 in front of Henry, who looked at and tried to grab the number stickers in both fists.

Use of Rhymes With Home Implements

Both Deaf mothers shared information with the other participants about their use at home of rhymes and variations on rhymes, and their children's responses to individual rhymes. Julia and Donna both reported that the ASL version of "Row, Row Your Boat" was most effective when both mother and baby were seated in a bathtub with real water. Jonathan first introduced this rhyme by stating that it was for hearing people but he had tried adapting it. He first demonstrated this rhyme with the doll (see figure 2):

> Jonathan sits with his doll resting against his bent knees. He signs RAIN falling rhythmically over the doll and then waves of water rising higher and higher on either side. The boat carrying the doll floats over the waves. Jonathan picks up the doll's arm and rows. Fish swim by on the left and right sides of the boat and then jump through the air. Jonathan and doll keep rowing. A fish soars through the air, into Jonathan's mouth and down his throat. His torso shakes and the doll shakes gently as Jonathan pounds his chest with one fist. The fish flies out of his mouth.

When the participants reviewed "Row, Row Your Boat," Donna noted that a bathtub setting for this rhyme provided support for the adult signer's back and legs. She advised Jonathan that a baby will also need some support for sitting up until he or she is about 10 months old. (Donna again suggested the bathtub as a suitable home setting when the participants later learned and reviewed the "Whale" rhyme.)

Julia reported using a version of "Elephant Looking for a Friend" at home, in which she used a picture of three monkeys to create a story about monkeys looking for a banana. Later she described using a mobile with a moon and stars when signing "Shining Star" at home with Henry and signing "Swing" when Henry was seated on a real swing in the park. Although the program does not use toys, books, or props, it appeared that Julia saw the use of concrete implements in conjunction with ASL rhymes as one way of supporting emergent ASL literacy at home and in the community. These examples from the Deaf mothers highlight context-bound, as distinct from context-independent, ASL literacy practices. The use of implements at home may also have come about because, as Donna reported, there were many more toys and objects in the Deaf mothers' home environments than in our program space at DSA. Donna described using a stuffed toy bear, tiger, and lion lined up in a row when signing

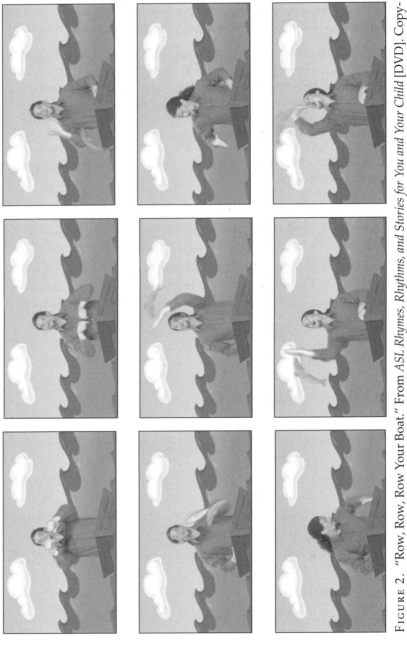

Figure 2. "Row, Row, Row Your Boat." From *ASL Rhymes, Rhythms, and Stories for You and Your Child* [DVD]. Copyright 2008 by the Ontario Cultural Society of the Deaf. Used with permission.

"Peekaboo Animals" at home with Violet, and a large stuffed bear when signing "Jolly Bear." She explained that Violet looked from Donna to the stuffed bear to herself when her mother signed this rhyme. At another point in our program, Donna commented that using a drum during rhymes worked well for increasing their tactile and vibratory components.

Modelling ASL Communication With Young Children

Throughout the program, the Deaf mothers modelled ASL communication with young children. Donna and Julia regularly signed with their children in free moments regarding the surrounding environment and what their children were doing. As Henry began teething midway through the program, Julia reported more difficulty with using rhymes for extended periods of time, although he still attended to several familiar rhymes that he preferred, including "Caterpillar." Julia explained that while Henry was teething, she was mainly able to sign rhymes and stories when her son was seated in his high chair and occupied with eating or drinking his bottle. Henry liked being rocked more often at this time, and Julia demonstrated for the other participants how she signed "Sleep and Dream" while holding and rocking her son. Henry had also become more prone to biting, and Julia explained that she often told her son that various items, such as a doll's nose or a human chin, hurt when he bit them.

Benefits to Deaf Mothers of Participation in the Program

Although the Deaf mothers in our program were already exceptionally qualified and well informed in regard to supporting young children's emergent language and literacy, they reported several benefits for both their children and themselves from participating in the program. In interviews following our 7th session, Donna noted that participating gave Violet more exposure to ASL literacy and enhanced language development. Violet also enjoyed socializing with the other children, and Donna herself appreciated the opportunity to participate in the community and share her knowledge and experience with the other mothers. Similarly, Julia reported that participation in the program greatly increased the amount of and frequency with which she signed rhymes and stories with Henry. Both Donna and Julia reported that the use of ASL rhymes was calming and enjoyable for their children.

Deaf Mothers' Interactions With Hearing Mothers and Their Children

Julia and Donna also modelled communication with the children of hearing parents. On several occasions, the Deaf mothers signed rhymes and stories with these children, such as when Julia signed "Dog Story" to David during the 7th program session. Like several other ASL rhymes and stories mentioned in this chapter, this story involves personification:

> Julia, with an animated expression, fingerspells the title "Dog Story," then signs DOG. Dog runs on clawed V classifier handshape limbs with her tongue hanging out. Dog stops and sniffs the air. Her tail shoots up and then points in the direction of the scent. Dog runs in the direction of the scent, stops, and digs up a bone.
> David watches Julia and smiles. Dog picks up the bone in her teeth and runs off.
> She stops and digs a hole, then drops the bone from her jaws. David sits still, watches Julia, and smiles. Dog brushes dirt over the hole and signs SHHH! to David, who watches Julia. SHHH! she signs again, looking around. Dog runs off again with her tongue hanging out.

The above story mainly uses the clawed V handshape (for the running dog) and the 1 and bent 1 handshapes (for the dog's tail, the bone, and the narrator's SHHH) as classifiers.

Julia and Donna also conversed with the children of hearing mothers, modelled attention-getting behaviors, and assisted the hearing mothers with learning rhymes. They frequently reminded the children of each other's name signs.

Advice to Other Mothers

As our program progressed and the participants grew familiar with each other, the Deaf mothers gave advice to the hearing mothers. At the beginning of the 5th program session, Julia told Grace about her participation with Henry in swimming lessons and in a baby sign program. Julia commented that she tried to go out with Henry as often as possible so that he could socialize with other young children. She felt that doing so enhanced Henry's development and confidence as he met different people and became involved with his community. Grace smiled and listened to Julia.

Similarly, before the start of our 6th session, as Bianca, Donna, and Julia were seated on the mat with their children, Julia asked Bianca if she knew how to tap her child's shoulder in order to get his attention. Julia then demonstrated tapping on Henry's shoulder. Henry turned and looked at his mother. Later during this session, I observed Bianca touching Charlie for attention and asking him, MORE? He reached for her hands as she signed to him. Bianca then signed to Charlie to look at Jonathan, who had resumed addressing the group.

During the last program session, Julia told the group about her practice of banging on the table or floor at home in order to get Henry's attention. Julia stomped her foot to demonstrate, and Charlie, who had crawled away from the group, turned his head to look. Julia commented that when Henry crawled away from her at home, she would likewise stomp her foot and wave for his attention. In the same session, Julia commented to Alison that she thought Tom was saying the word "Mama." Julia then signed MOTHER to Tom. In response, Alison told Julia that Tom frequently called out and sang, "Mom, Mom." Julia advised Alison that she could respond to Tom in ASL by signing MOTHER. As she remarked, Henry also sometimes made the lip movements for "Mama" and Julia then signed MOTHER back to him. Julia stated that doing so helped Henry to learn the names of people and objects, and how to express himself.

Donna advised other Deaf and hearing parents about the use of hearing aids. During the 5th program session, Donna's attention was caught by a conversation taking place between Peter and Mary about Sarah's hearing aids. Donna asked Mary about what Mary had said, and Mary explained that her daughter wore hearing aids but did not seem to like them and tended to pull them off. Donna remarked that Sarah was not ready to wear hearing aids and should not be forced. She advised Peter and Mary that Sarah wanted to be comfortable—if she pulled off her hearing aids, it meant she was not comfortable. Donna added that Sarah may become more used to her hearing aids later, as some of Donna's students had. Her students sometimes wanted to wear their hearing aids. The following week, as Bianca was conversing with a DSA staff member about Charlie's hearing aids being lost, Donna interjected that many parents have problems with children losing their hearing aids. As she told Bianca, this was more likely to happen when children were younger than the age of 7. Bianca protested to Donna, "But I was holding him! His hearing aid just fell off." Donna commented that for young children, hearing aids were like shoes—they can be lost in minutes.

Donna's remarks about hearing aids indicate a certain practical, commonsense view of hearing loss and hearing technology that in part counterbalances the medical discourse regarding Deaf individuals that is discussed in the previous chapter. The role and contributions of hearing mothers in our program, as well as the role of the program leader, further illustrate this counterdiscourse regarding Deaf identity and the effects of hearing loss.

Hearing Mothers as Problem-Posers

Because of the context of Ontario infant hearing screening and early intervention services and the overall lack of support for the hearing mothers' use of ASL with their children, the fact of their participation in the program meant these mothers had already taken a distinct, active role. This context led the hearing mothers to assume a position of critical inquiry in regard to ASL and the issue of a Deaf identity. As they participated in the Deaf cultural space of our program and asked questions of the Deaf adult participants, these mothers embodied Freire's concept of problem-posing education, in which "the students—no longer docile listeners—are now critical co-investigators in dialogue with the teacher" (2000, p. 81).

Asking Questions of Deaf Adult Participants

During our 2nd program session, when she was the only hearing adult present beside the interpreter, Alison asked a question that indicated her regard for the knowledge of the Deaf adults. Holding Tom in her lap, she asked: "Because you have experience with kids who have hearing problems, I'm wondering if kids with hearing problems tend to scream more?" She smiled while she asked this question, then added: "I don't mean crying. He's happy, but more loud than other kids." Julia responded to Alison first:

> A Deaf baby is trying to hear himself. He is playing with his voice and screaming for fun because he can't hear anything. It's very loud. If the baby could hear himself, it would be different, but right now he doesn't fully understand. Henry is very loud and my mother tells me that it was the same when I was a baby. I let Henry scream if he wants to. If everyone turns to look, I don't mind. People will start to laugh. It's OK—let him be that way.

Donna was the next to answer Alison. Drawing on her professional experience, Donna explained that she teaches junior kindergarten at a Deaf school:

> Many kids in my class scream. It's natural for Deaf kids to do this— they can't hear themselves. Julia is right about kids playing with their voices. They will experiment with making different sounds. You can feel your own voice even if you don't hear it. Babbling with voices and hands occurs in the same way—it's natural. If you try to shush your baby, he won't understand.

Julia also suggested that Alison could try responding to Tom when he yelled:

> If you're holding Tom and he screams, then you can pretend to be startled. Try communicating with Tom—you can hum while holding him and he will feel your voice. You can respond to your baby's sounds in various ways [Julia picked up Henry who had started to cry. She then demonstrated the various sounds, such as humming, that she could make while holding Henry.] Your baby can feel your voice when you hold him, and it calms him down. Eventually, your baby will understand about sounds and voices.

In the above conversation, the Deaf mothers had further opportunity to convey a normalizing, noncatastrophic view of young Deaf children and their behaviors. They also made practical suggestions for how Alison might turn an instance of her son's yelling into an opportunity for learning and fostering communication. However, this discussion and the approaches to Deaf identity that it revealed took place in part because of Alison's role as an inquirer.

When I interviewed Alison following the end of our 6th session and asked if she had any suggestions for improving our program, she again expressed curiosity about Deaf people and their approaches to hearing technology:

> I have some questions relating to Deaf culture. I would really like to have time to ask questions and discuss that. It would be cool if we could do that. But I know that maybe all of the mothers may not be interested in the same questions—some are hearing and some are Deaf.

I assured Alison that she could ask any questions she wanted, and Jonathan, who had come up to us during our conversation, agreed. Alison continued: "Tom will get a hearing aid and I'm curious about how other kids deal with something like that. And Deaf culture—does it hate hearing aids or are they OK? Do they accept hearing aids?" I responded to Alison that many Deaf people wear hearing aids. Jonathan agreed and added:

It doesn't hurt to try hearing aids. Some Deaf people like to hear when there's a knock at the door or another noise. It can be hard to catch every word that is said in spoken conversation—I don't know if this is possible. Usually Deaf people need to make eye contact and lipread when using their residual hearing. It's not like with hearing people who can turn their heads away but still hear and understand everything.

Jonathan then added that there are some Deaf people he knows who can speak and hear well and who use the telephone.

Similarly, before the start of our 5th program session, I observed a conversation between Grace and Julia in which Grace asked about Julia's use of hearing technology for Henry. Grace asked Julia if Henry wore hearing aids, and Julia explained that he did not; she felt the degree of Henry's hearing loss meant that hearing aids would not be useful for him. Grace then asked Julia about a cochlear implant for Henry. Julia answered that she would not choose an implant for him—from looking at her own life and her husband's, she knows that Henry will be fine without one.

The space provided by our program seemed to enable the asking and answering of questions about the Deaf adults' perspectives on Deaf identity and hearing technology. Following our 6th session and Alison's question about hearing aids, a group discussion began about early intervention services and cochlear implants. Bianca and Alison both stated that they were committed to learning ASL but found it difficult to obtain support for doing so. At this time, Bianca remarked that no matter what, she wanted Charlie to be part of the Deaf community.

Jonathan and the other participants then shared their views about cochlear implants. Jonathan said that many Deaf children with cochlear implants end up learning ASL and joining the Deaf community when they grow up. He mentioned that there are students with cochlear implants at provincial schools for Deaf students who arrive with low language skills because of not being allowed to learn ASL. Alison then remarked that all the books she had read told her that learning ASL does not hinder speech development, although this is the opposite of what she was told by her son's doctor. (This statement by Alison is similar to the comment that Bianca reported making to the speech-language pathologist during Charlie's first AVT session.)

Approaches to Learning ASL

As evidenced by Bianca and Alison's remarks, the hearing mothers took a critical, active approach to the issues of Deaf children's bilingualism and learning of ASL. While conversing with Alison during our 2nd program session, I asked her if she had started using ASL rhymes at home with her husband and Tom. Alison replied in the affirmative and then told me that she and her husband regularly used six different signs when communicating with Tom: MOTHER, FATHER, FOOD/EAT, HELLO, GOODBYE, I LOVE YOU (with the combined LY handshape). Alison then said that now that she was learning more ASL, she planned to teach Tom more signs.

The hearing mothers also took an active approach in learning and using ASL vocabulary and rhymes and in asking questions about ASL. By the 2nd week of our program, Alison reported that Tom liked "Peekaboo Animals" the most of the rhymes she had begun using with him. She also stated that he immediately recognized this rhyme whenever she signed it, regardless of whether she was standing at a distance or seated close to Tom. Alison made sure that her comments were included in the review sessions that Jonathan led each week, where the parents shared information regarding their use of rhymes at home and their children's responses. For example, during our 3rd session when Jonathan asked the participants about their use of the rhymes they had learned the previous week, Alison was the first to answer: She had tried using "Row, Row Your Boat" in the bathtub with Tom, who enjoyed this activity very much. In this and other instances, Alison also demonstrated her receptivity to the suggestions and example of the Deaf mothers who had mentioned using this rhyme in the bathtub.

Bianca also demonstrated an active approach to learning ASL, as when she asked me how to sign that she will feed Charlie. I involved Julia in this conversation, and Julia showed Bianca the vocabulary about eating that she used with Henry. Bianca then practiced signing that Charlie was hungry and it was time to eat. Bianca took several opportunities to interact and sign with the Deaf mothers and Deaf child participants, as when Henry and Charlie played together during the 6th program session. As Henry brushed Charlie's face with his hand, Bianca tapped Henry's shoulder and told him to be gentler. Like Alison, Bianca also reported on her use of rhymes and stories at home with Charlie. For example, during our last session Bianca noted that signing "Bird and Worm" while Charlie was eating helped him become more interested in his food.

Grace asked questions about ASL and the content of the program. It was clear that the concept of an ASL poem was new to her, and she lacked some of the background knowledge about ASL that the other hearing mothers brought with them. During our 3rd week, when Jonathan introduced "Sandwich," Grace asked me if the rhyme was from ASL or English. I explained to her that it was from ASL and there was no real English translation for the rhyme. However, it appears that I gave Grace inaccurate information. "Sandwich" is said to be a traditional Irish rhyme, although the original source is unknown. Another ASL Parent-Child Mother Goose Program leader, who introduced this rhyme when the program was founded, explains that her hearing father signed "Sandwich" with her when she was very young. Her father employed various ASL handshapes while also fingerspelling the various sandwich components (butter, salt, meat). It seems that her father had adapted a version of this rhyme, which he had learned from his own mother, for signing with his Deaf daughter (S. Pollock, personal communication, January 20, 2009).

Grace also asked several questions about the meaning of various ASL vocabulary items, such as when during our 3rd session she separately asked Jonathan and me about the meaning of the combined LY handshape in "ILY Balloon." On several occasions, instead of trying to sign a new rhyme herself, Grace asked either Jonathan or me to sign rhymes with David while she watched us. It appeared that our program was sometimes too fast-paced for Grace to fully learn all of the rhymes and stories when they were first introduced. However, by the 5th and 7th sessions Grace reported using "Jolly Bear," "Fall," "Hungry, Eat Your Toes," and several other rhymes at home with David. She also described David's responses to certain rhymes.

Benefits to Hearing Mothers of Participation in Our Program

The hearing mothers reported various benefits from participating in the program. Alison mentioned the calming effects that her use of rhymes had for Tom. Bianca described riding the subway with Charlie in his stroller and signing "Jolly Bear" and "Whale" to keep him "happy in a quiet way." Grace stated of the program:

> It's really nice, and it's another kind of play for us. Another way of playing a game. It helps with interaction and our relationship. It helps us play—you know, we have other games at home that we play with David, so it's like an addition to these. It's nice and something I really like.

Following the end of our program at DSA, I learned from Jonathan and other individuals that Alison continued to attend both a subsequent ASL Parent-Child Mother Goose Program and a parent ASL class taught by Julia at DSA. Although there were few resources for supporting the hearing parents' learning of ASL during the tenure of our program, our program appeared to lead to more parent-focused ASL activities being initiated at DSA. Bianca, who like Grace had returned to work from maternity leave, had finally started to receive ASL and literacy consultant services.

The Program Leader as Facilitator of Emergent ASL Literacy

In his role as ASL Parent-Child Mother Goose Program leader and creator of several ASL rhymes and stories for young children, Jonathan was at the center of an emerging children's ASL literature tradition. Due to a lack of preexisting resources, both Deaf and hearing parents are often unlikely to have significant experience with ASL literature activities for young children. Through his work as program leader, Jonathan aimed at teaching and further developing various ASL rhymes and stories and fostering emergent ASL literacy and the acquisition of an ASL discourse by parents and children.

Noticing Child Response

From the start of our program, Jonathan called the other participants' attention to children's various responses to ASL rhymes. Along with visual attention, child response appears to be central to defining emergent ASL literacy in young children. Jonathan's first comment regarding child response followed Julia's use of "Peekaboo Animals" with Henry during our 1st session. Julia signed the rhyme:

> PEEKABOO! LION, LION.
> PEEKABOO! TIGER, TIGER.
> PEEKABOO! BEAR, BEAR
> PEEKABOO! MONKEY, MONKEY.
> PEEKABOO! Julia signed a SPIDER that crawls forward over baby.

This rhyme involves the extended B handshape for PEEKABOO and the clawed spread C handshape for various animal signs. These animal signs employ locations that move from the crown of the head (as in LION) to the lower half of the face (as in TIGER) to the shoulders (as in BEAR) to the sides of the torso (as in MONKEY), then out and away from the adult signer with the sign for SPIDER (see figure 3). Henry with arms outstretched kicked his legs in response while his mother signed to him. Tom beside him also made leg movements as Alison signed the rhyme.

FIGURE 3. "Peekaboo Animals." From *The ASL Parent-Child Mother Goose Program: American Sign Language Rhymes, Rhythms and Stories for Parents and Their Children* [DVD]. Copyright 2004 by the Ontario Cultural Society of the Deaf. Used with permission.

At this time, Jonathan commented about excitatory arm and leg movements that signal child response. As he stated during our 3rd session, these kicking and arm and hand movements are the start of communication between parent and child. He noted that child facial expression was also in evidence, as with the infants' opening and closing mouths in response to this rhyme.

At various times, Jonathan called the adult participants' attention to the responses made by individual children and encouraged parents to analyze their children's responses to rhymes. When reviewing participating parents' use of rhymes from the previous week, Jonathan frequently asked the mothers how their children had responded. During our 2nd session, Jonathan noted that Violet's response to ASL rhymes was evident in her facial expression. When Grace and David arrived during our 3rd session and Jonathan signed "Peekaboo Animals" to David for the first time, he commented that David watched him quietly and seemed fascinated, then responded to the rhyme by smiling. Jonathan later observed that David, who had less exposure to ASL than the other children, also made less eye contact and had less visual attention when he started attending our program. However, by subsequent sessions, David's visual attention and response to rhymes had improved.

Jonathan had seen Charlie with his father at a DSA family event and signed "Shining Star" to them. Charlie giggled in response to Jonathan signing shining stars in his eyes and using an index finger to outline his face. During a later program session, when he taught the rhyme "Sleep and Dream," Jonathan commented to Bianca that Charlie enjoyed rhymes where his face was touched by an adult signer, and Bianca agreed. At the end of this session, Jonathan advised Bianca and Julia: "First sign to your baby, then stop and wait. There will be a bodily response from your baby, such as kicking. Sign, then wait—your baby will respond to you. This is part of communication and developing language." For example, Henry had kicked vigorously that day during the "I Love You, Bye" circle, which meant, "Come on, I want more." Charlie had a different response to this rhyme: He rolled over both times the parent participants signed it. Jonathan remarked to Bianca that her use of rhymes at home with Charlie would encourage his language development and enhance his ability to express himself and participate in the turn-taking of communication; Bianca responded that Charlie had started to copy various handshapes from signs she used with him.

Child response to certain rhymes increased as the children grew familiar with the rhymes' content and structure. For example, following Jonathan's introduction of "Bird and Worm" during our 5th session, Julia mentioned her use at home of the conceptually similar rhyme, "Hungry, Eat Your Toes." In "Bird and Worm," the adult signer describes a bird in its nest that looks outward, spots a worm on the ground, then descends with a flapping of its wings. The bird then plucks and pretends to swallow the fingers of a child's hand, one by one, as if they were worms. As Jonathan demonstrated this rhyme, the last finger of the child's hand is difficult to pluck and results in a struggle for the bird. In "Hungry, Eat Your Toes," the adult signs that he or she is hungry and pretends to pluck and swallow a child's fingers or toes, one by one. Julia shared that Henry laughed and pulled his hand back in anticipation when she signed this latter rhyme, as he had grown familiar with its structure. Similarly, Donna reported that Violet giggled in anticipation when her mother began signing "Peekaboo Animals" at home, because Violet knew that the spider was coming to tickle her at the end. Alison added that Tom also smiled in anticipation of the spider during the same rhyme.

Improvising and Revising ASL Rhymes and Encouraging the Use of Rhymes With Other Family Members

Jonathan emphasized for the parents that they could be creative in making additions and revisions to rhymes. Following Julia's demonstration of "Peekaboo Animals," Jonathan showed an alternate version of the rhyme, in which the adult signer stands and adds walking movements for each animal sign to create personification: The feline lion and tiger prowl, the bear dances with forepaws waving, the monkey swings its arms, and the spider crawls forward. Jonathan suggested that this alternate version could be used with older children.

He and Julia then demonstrated "Peekaboo Animals Line-Up," in which two adult partners sign the rhyme in a turn-taking sequence. The first adult signer begins: PEEKABOO! LION, LION. Then the first adult moves aside to stand behind the second, who in turn steps forward to sign PEEKABOO! TIGER, TIGER. The second adult steps aside and the first signer steps forward to resume: PEEKABOO! BEAR, BEAR. The first adult again steps aside and the second steps forward: PEEKABOO! MONKEY, MONKEY. At the end both adults together sign PEEKABOO! then SPIDERS crawling over the child. In response to Jonathan and Julia's signing of this rhyme, Henry waved his arms and kicked his legs in a cycling motion. Julia shared that Henry tended to wave his arms in a horizontal motion when he was asked, MORE? When the participants reviewed "Peekaboo Animals Line-Up" 1 week later, Julia demonstrated a different version of this rhyme, in which she turned around once after each animal sign instead of forming a line-up with a partner.

Jonathan introduced "Rollercoaster" as another rhyme that could be signed at home with a husband or other adult partner to encourage communication and foster children's visual attention. Jonathan suggested that one adult partner could clap the rhythm while the other lifted the child in the movement of a rollercoaster.

During our 3rd session Jonathan introduced "Elephant Looking for a Friend" and again suggested different ways in which parents could be creative with using rhymes. As he demonstrated,

Elephant searches and searches for a friend, lifts baby's arm, and looks. Elephant searches, searches, and lifts baby's other arm to look. Elephant's trunk waves from left to right. Elephant looks under baby's left, then right leg. [Jonathan shows the parents how they should roll their eyes from left to right when signing SEARCH to indicate they are looking for something.]

Jonathan suggested using versions of rhymes that ranged from the simple to the complex, according to the parents' signing skills. Jonathan told Grace to try signing "Elephant Looking for a Friend" with David. However, Grace asked him to again tell her how the rhyme went. Jonathan considered, and then announced he would show the group another version:

> Elephant begins searching. His trunk waves from left to right. He's looking for a friend—hmm! Where could one be? His trunk waves from left to right. There—that's an easy version to use.

Jonathan added that the parents could sign this rhyme when their child was seated in his or her high chair. He demonstrated how a parent could walk with his or her elephant's trunk swinging and by stomping his or her feet rhythmically. At the end when a friend is found, the parent could skip forward in delight with trunk waving and hug his or her child. For the hearing mothers' benefit, Jonathan also introduced both more complex and simpler versions of "Crocodile" when this rhyme was introduced during our 7th session.

Like the Deaf mothers, Jonathan demonstrated various tactile and vibratory strategies for retaining a child's visual attention. As he continued to discuss variations for "Elephant Looking for a Friend," Jonathan signed the rhyme with David:

> Jonathan bangs his trunk on the floor to get David's attention. His trunk waves from left to right and pats David as he searches. David watches Jonathan and smiles as the elephant searches and searches for a friend. Jonathan points to David—it's you!—and thumps forward to pat David enthusiastically with his trunk. David smiles in response and Jonathan gently tickles him.

Creation of ASL Literacy and Numeracy Activities

Like the Deaf mothers, Jonathan suggested various ASL literacy and numeracy activities for the parents to try with their children.

As Bianca fed Charlie some pureed fruit during a break in our 4th session, Jonathan sat in front of them and began signing:

> Jonathan signs 2 spoonfuls, 3 spoonfuls going into his own mouth as Charlie and Bianca watch. 4 spoonfuls, 5 spoonfuls—all done! Jonathan leans toward Charlie and counts on Jonathan's own fingers with ASL numbers: 1, 2, 3, 4, 5, FINISHED.
>
> Holding Charlie's fist, Jonathan then begins counting on Charlie's fingers, then signs EAT, EAT, FINISHED! MORE? Charlie watches Jonathan as Bianca continues to feed him spoonfuls. Bianca asks Charlie, MORE? and Charlie waves his hand.

Another episode occurred during our last session when Charlie was eating a snack of dry Cheerios cereal. Jonathan waved for everyone's attention and announced that he had created a song using Cheerios. With his base or nondominant hand, he used the F handshape as a classifier for a Cheerio. Using his dominant hand, a 1 handshape shot up rapidly as Jonathan pretended to pop a Cheerio into his mouth. He continued signing 2, 3, 4, 5 Cheerios as he pretended to eat.

Facilitating Awareness of ASL

Jonathan used his teaching of various ASL rhymes and stories as opportunities to enhance participants' understanding of ASL and its structure. For example, during our 2nd session Jonathan mentioned the title of the rhyme "Jolly Bear" and how in ASL, the adjective usually follows the noun (i.e., the ASL translation for this rhyme's title is BEAR JOLLY). He also remarked that with this rhyme, the signer needs to make clear that he or she is signing about a bear before describing the bear's various features (as when signing BEAR before the bear's big ears, puffy cheeks, and jolly tummy). Here Jonathan made reference to the use of depicting verbs (also called classifier predicates), which are morphological structures in ASL. With these structures, the noun is signed first, then the depicting verb is used to state something about the noun (Lucas, Valli, Mulrooney, & Villanueva, 2011). With Peter and Mary, who primarily used LSM, Jonathan frequently provided explanations of ASL vocabulary items and their corresponding English translation for the notes that Peter regularly made when he participated in our program.

Facilitating ASL Literacy with Individual Parents

Jonathan regularly worked with the individual parent participants to enhance their use of individual rhymes. During our 3rd session, Jonathan introduced "How Much I Love You." As he demonstrated this rhyme with Violet:

> I love you with a tiny little heart? Jonathan thinks and decides not. I love you with a good-sized, medium heart? Jonathan thinks and decides not, with a frown. I love you with a great big enormous heart? That big? Yes! Jonathan then demonstrates how the adult signer can pick up and hug his or her child.

Following his demonstration, Jonathan went over to where Alison and Tom were sitting on the mat and practicing the new rhyme. Alison signed the "No" parts of the rhyme, where the signer decides that a particular size of heart is inaccurate, with shakes of her head. Tom held his arms outstretched and sucked on his pacifier as he watched his mother sign. Alison animatedly signed a great big heart at the end of the rhyme and Tom waved his right arm in response. Jonathan told Alison that she had done a great job. He then provided Alison with the following instructions for signing the rhyme:

> For the first heart, think small. Add facial expression to show you're thinking about the size of the heart. Roll your eyes as you ponder—babies like facial expression. Tilt your head and put your finger on your chin to show you're thinking. You can shake your head "No" after you decide about the size of the first and second heart. Use facial expression when making a decision about the first, second, and third hearts. For the last heart, decide "Yes!" with excitement.

Alison watched Jonathan and nodded as he demonstrated. She then signed the rhyme again with much more facial expression, and Tom started waving his arms and kicking excitedly in response. Jonathan praised Alison's efforts. During our last session, Jonathan increased the tactile components of this rhyme by moving Tom's arms through the motions of the three different hearts. (He employed the same strategy of moving a child's arms for several other rhymes in our program.) Jonathan then demonstrated to Alison how she could continue to hold Tom's arms as she shook her head "No" after the first and second hearts, and then nodded "Yes" after the third heart. Doing so caused Tom's body to rock gently as Alison shook her head, and kept his visual attention trained on his mother.

Similarly, during our 4th session, Jonathan introduced "Dog Story" to Charlie and Bianca and scaffolded Bianca's learning of the story. He first signed the story to Charlie, whose eyes followed Jonathan's movements as Jonathan's dog spotted and picked up a bone, then dropped the bone into a hole and covered it with dirt. Jonathan then explained the various components of "Dog Story" to Bianca and told her to try signing the story. As I held Charlie in my lap, Jonathan and Bianca together practiced signing "Dog Story." Charlie laughed and waved his arms as the dogs' tails shot up, and he waved his arms again as both dogs spotted and picked up their bones, dug holes to bury them, dropped their bones into the holes, and signed SHH to Charlie. Here Charlie brought his own index finger up to his face in imitation of the adults' gestures. The dogs ran off and Charlie laughed again. One week later, when I observed Bianca independently signing this story with Charlie, he responded in recognition of what she was doing. His eyes followed Bianca's movements as she dug a hole for the dog's bone. Charlie then held out his arms, shook his head, and laughed with delight.

Whereas Jonathan sometimes employed the services of the ASL interpreter when working with individual hearing mothers, on several occasions he instructed the interpreter to stop talking while he demonstrated various rhymes. By doing so, he worked to support the mothers' receptive skills. Jonathan also modelled attention-getting behaviors by tapping the hearing mothers' shoulders for attention when he wanted to make a comment.

Differences Between Deaf and Hearing Parents

Jonathan led different ASL Parent-Child Mother Goose Programs with two different participant groups, and he occasionally commented on differences he observed between Deaf and hearing parents when learning and using ASL rhymes. During our 2nd session, after Alison described Tom's preference for "Peekaboo Animals," Jonathan commented that hearing parents and children always seemed to like this particular rhyme, perhaps due to its relative simplicity. At our 5th session, as he explained several variations for "Shining Star," Jonathan remarked that Deaf parents are experts in creating variations for ASL rhymes, just as hearing parents find it easy to play with and creatively manipulate their own first, spoken language, but hearing parents who are learning ASL can practice and make progress with using ASL rhymes. However, as Jonathan remarked during our 2nd session, the Deaf and hearing babies whom he taught responded to ASL rhymes in the same way.

In an interview with Jonathan 3 weeks after our program began at DSA, I asked him about the differences he noticed between programs with hearing and Deaf participants. He replied that he felt that the ASL Parent-Child Mother Goose Program was best suited for ASL-fluent Deaf parents of hearing and Deaf children. With this participant group, he was always learning new improvisations and techniques that improved his own practice as a program leader. Hearing parents, who often have no foundation in ASL—such as the group of hearing parents and children who attended the alternate program that Jonathan led—may require a different approach. This participant group of parents often did not make eye contact or pay visual attention to him, making leading a program much more challenging. Jonathan later remarked again on the difficulty of teaching rhymes and stories to parents who lacked prior knowledge of ASL.

Through these interviews and in the course of my study, it emerged that the ASL Parent-Child Mother Goose Program, as the only free resource for supporting parents and children's learning of ASL, was sometimes required to take on a role for which it was not intended. As the program leader, Jonathan did not see it as his responsibility to teach basic ASL vocabulary to parents who had no previous knowledge of the language. His real aim was supporting the learning of ASL rhymes and stories and further developing such ASL literacy resources for young children.

Suggestions for Improvement

Within its action research format, our program included several opportunities for participants to make suggestions for improved practice. Some ASL rhymes and stories that Jonathan introduced were newly created and still in the process of development, for example, "Moon":

> Using the extended C handshape, Jonathan signs a MOON high in the sky.
>
> Jonathan looks at his doll's face and, using the Y handshape, signs SAME! between the baby's face and the moon. Using the 1 handshape, he points out 1, 2 eyes on the moon, then 1, 2 eyes on himself, then 1, 2, eyes on baby. Jonathan gasps with surprise and again signs SAME! between the baby's face and the moon. He then points out 1, 2 eyes, then a nose on the moon, himself, and baby, and again signs SAME! between baby's face and the moon. He repeats this sequence with 1, 2 eyes then a nose and an arc for the mouth on the moon, his own face, and his doll's face. Jonathan ends the rhyme by again signing a MOON high in the sky.

Jonathan made several starts and stops when signing "Moon" as he worked out the correct sequence. As he remarked to Julia at this time, he did not feel satisfied with this rhyme and wished to develop more detail. He also stated that he felt the concept of a MOON in the sky may be too abstract for a very young child. Following a suggestion I made, Jonathan agreed that a doll's face could be used instead of an abstract moon, but added that (aside from the doll that he sometimes used to demonstrate rhymes) during the ASL Parent-Child Mother Goose Program no toys or other objects are used. As Jonathan remarked, if a parent was grocery shopping with his or her child, the parent may not have a doll handy for signing this rhyme. Jonathan then suggested that another adult partner's face could be used instead of a MOON.

It was clear in the course of our program that several parents required repeated demonstrations of some rhymes and stories. Our program sometimes appeared to attempt to cover too many rhymes each week in a too-rapid sequence. However, as I remarked in a follow-up interview with Jonathan after our program at DSA ended, the original Parent-Child Mother Goose Program is 30 weeks in length. If 30 weeks were also allotted for the ASL Parent-Child Mother Goose Program, then there would be much more time and space for learning and practicing ASL rhymes and stories. The lack of public resources for hosting ASL Parent-Child Mother Goose Programs seems to be linked to the difficulty that Jonathan reported in leading programs with hearing adult participants who did not have other support for learning ASL.

In addition, although Jonathan suggested that the participating parents make notes of rhymes and stories on the handouts with program schedules that he distributed each week, I did not observe any parents other than Peter taking notes. (As Peter attended our program with his wife, one parent was free to attend to Sarah as the other took notes.) Grace suggested during our last interview that providing a simple, written explanation of rhymes and stories would help her remember how to use them. At the end of our program I presented participants with copies of the *ASL Parent-Child Mother Goose Program* DVD, which includes examples of several ASL rhymes (a second DVD with additional rhymes has since been published), but these resources were not otherwise free to parents participating in our program.

On several occasions when I interviewed Donna, she suggested that 5 or 10 minutes of our program sessions should be allotted for the hearing parents to ask questions about Deaf culture. She mentioned name signs and Deaf babies' yelling as potential topics for discussion.

Finally, Jonathan was not satisfied with the mid-afternoon time frame for our program, since it conflicted with naptime for several children. He felt that the morning or later in the afternoon were better times, because the children would be more rested and alert. Several parents agreed with Jonathan's suggestion.

In my final interview with Jonathan, we discussed these suggestions for improvement in relation to future programs that Jonathan planned to host in the next year. We also discussed the need for further resources for supporting ASL learning and literacy in parents and Deaf children.

8

Conclusion

THE DEAF MOTHER participants' and program leader's use of ASL rhymes and ASL literacy activities in the ASL Parent-Child Mother Goose program work toward a definition of emergent ASL literacy in very young children. Two central parts of this definition are visual attentiveness and response. In very young children, response to a visual language takes the form of excitatory arm and leg movements, hand and vocal babbling, and laughing, smiling, and other types of affect. In addition, the program's teaching and repetition of ASL rhymes support children's anticipation of rhyme sequences as a feature of response. The presence of manual babbling, such as occurred in some of the child participants' production of certain handshapes, is distinct from excitatory motor hand activity that occurs in all infants, and is a key feature of infant babbling in infants exposed to natural signed languages (Petitto, 2000; Petitto & Marentette, 1991). Early intervention programs for Deaf children and their parents should incorporate ASL literature—poems and stories like those featured in this book—as a vital means of supporting young children's visual attention, response, and language development. In addition to signing rhymes and stories with children, resources in the form of ASL literature DVDs are a way for parents to support emergent ASL literacy at home.

The ways in which the Deaf adult participants in the program fostered emergent ASL literacy through use of ASL rhymes and stories, and particularly through their extensive use of revisions and improvisations to existing rhymes, may indicate some distinctive features of ASL poetry as a genre of ASL literature. In

116

ASL Poetry: Selected Works of Clayton Valli (Valli, 1995), Marlon Kuntze remarks that ASL poetry is a more recent phenomenon than ASL itself due to historical oppression of the language, and ASL poetry is still expanding and developing as a genre. Hence, a complete understanding of ASL poetry and its differences from spoken or written poetry may still be a work in progress. The constant variation in how ASL rhymes were signed with the young children in my study may be a unique feature of ASL poetry use with children who are in the process of acquiring receptive skills in a signed language. This feature also suggests some possible differences between the respective functions of spoken-language nursery rhymes and ASL rhymes in terms of supporting literacy in a spoken and signed language, and indicates that further study may be needed regarding whether variation in signed language poetry differs from how spoken-language rhymes are used with young children. These forms of literacy and literature are often thought to be synonymous with orality and oral literature (Bahan, 1991). *Orality* is defined by its use of myth and storytelling; rhyme, rhythm, and meter; metaphor; and literary events involving participation by a speaker and listener (Egan, 1987). Both the spoken-language and ASL Parent-Child Mother Goose Program can be said to involve the elements of orality, but the latter program incorporates these features in a way that supports learning of a visual language.

ASL Literacy Resources

Future research on emergent ASL literacy should investigate programs and services in a policy context that incorporates broad support for Deaf children's bilingualism in a signed and spoken/written language. It seems clear that some of the processes and outcomes of a family ASL literacy program with Deaf and hearing parents and children may be different given adequate support for Deaf children and their parents' participation in ASL programs and ASL literature activities. In particular, in the case of our program, the hearing parents may have been better able to benefit from the program leader's teaching of rhymes and stories if they had other, concurrent support for learning ASL. Additionally, the program leader's practice may have differed substantially if he were more free to teach a range of rhymes and stories without undue concern for hearing parents' knowledge of ASL. Given such a context, I envision future studies undertaken on a wider scale and with larger numbers of participants and programs. Additionally, longitudinal studies of young children exposed to family ASL programs and services could track their ASL literacy and bilingual development over time.

As I outlined in Chapter 2, it is precisely their lack of access to ASL and an ASL discourse that leaves so many Deaf children at a disadvantage when they begin school. The poetic and storytelling techniques of orality as conveyed in the ASL Parent-Child Mother Goose Program are frequently absent in the impoverished linguistic environment faced by many young Deaf children. Public services to Deaf children and their families that include greater support for learning ASL from Deaf adult professionals and for participation in ASL literature programs should be viewed as a support for bilingual development. An early intervention framework in which speech and hearing professionals work cooperatively with Deaf adult providers of ASL services will better ensure that the needs of Deaf children and their families are truly served.

Another implication of my findings derives from the ways in which Deaf and hearing adults worked collaboratively in the context of our program. In Sweden, a network formed of Deaf organizations, a national organization of parents of Deaf children, and academics helped to effect policy reform and systemic changes for supporting signed language and bilingual education programs (Mahshie, 1995). Other studies have reported the potency of collaborative relations between Deaf and hearing parents of Deaf children for transforming hearing parents' perceptions of their children's identities and capabilities, enhancing the language learning and socialization of Deaf children, and creating an activist movement to ensure that all Deaf children receive the benefits of interaction with other Deaf children and adults (cited in Davies, 1991; Mahshie, 1995). Further support and opportunities for interaction between Deaf and hearing parents may point to another way that an ASL discourse can contain the seeds for transformative action.

Although the Deaf community's contributions are frequently overlooked by mainstream media and academic discourses, any country's historical and cultural landscape loses vibrancy if the languages, knowledge, and traditions of its Deaf community are subtracted. More importantly, in the 21st century young Deaf students' access to Deaf community discourses is in keeping with current understanding of the role of negotiating a positive social identity and an empowering education in fostering academic success (Cummins, 2001). Given its significant cognitive, affective, and academic benefits, young Deaf children's acquisition of a fully accessible, native signed language is a key matter of public interest. Government programs and services that work to restrict access to signed language for Deaf children and their families therefore must be held up to scrutiny and revised to fit a best-practices model of early bilingual education. Those public services that allocate what Lo Bianco (2001) terms a "multiple capital endowment" for native signed languages as primary languages of Deaf children will advance more progressive views and educational practices that are in the interest of both Deaf students and the public at large.

Bibliography

Abrahamsen, A. (2000). Explorations of enhanced gestural input to children in the bimodal period. In K. Emmorey & H. Lane (Eds.), *The signs of language revisited: An anthology to honor Ursula Bellugi and Edward Klima* (pp. 357–399). Hillsdale, NJ: Lawrence Erlbaum Associates.

Akamatsu C., Musselman, C., & Zweibel, A. (2000). Nature versus nurture in the development of cognition in deaf people. In P. Spencer, C. Erting, & M. Marschark (Eds.), *The deaf child in the family and the school: Essays in honour of Kathryn P. Meadow-Orlans* (pp. 255–274). Mahwah, NJ: Lawrence Erlbaum Associates.

Anderson, D. (2006). Lexical development of deaf children acquiring signed languages. In B. Schick, M. Marschark, & P. Spencer (Eds.), *Advances in the sign language development of deaf children* (pp. 135–160). New York: Oxford University Press.

Antia, S., & Kreimeyer, K. (2003). Peer interaction of deaf and hard-of-hearing children. In M. Marschark, & P. Spencer (Eds.), *Oxford handbook of deaf studies, language, and education* (pp. 164–176). New York: Oxford University Press.

Apuzzo, M., & Yoshinaga-Itano, C. (1995). Early identification of infants with significant hearing loss and the Minnesota Child Development Inventory. *Seminars in Hearing, 16,* 124–137.

Arehart, K., & Yoshinaga-Itano, C. (1999). The role of educators of the deaf in the early identification of hearing loss. *American Annals of the Deaf, 144*(1), 19–24.

Arehart, K., Yoshinaga-Itano, C., Thomson, V., Gabbard, S., & Stredler-Brown, A. (1998). State of the states: The status of universal newborn hearing identification and intervention systems in 16 states. *American Journal of Audiology, 7*(2), 101–114.

Bahan, B. (1991). ASL literature: Inside the story. *Proceedings of the Deaf Studies: What's Up? Conference* (pp. 153–164). Washington, DC: College for Continuing Education, Gallaudet University.

Bailey, C., & Dolby, K. (Eds.) (2002). *The Canadian Dictionary of ASL*. Edmonton, Alberta, Canada: University of Alberta Press.

Barab, S., Thomas, M., Dodge, T., Squire, K., & Newell, M. (2004). Critical design ethnography: Designing for change. *Anthropology & Education Quarterly, 35*(2), 254–268.

Bauman, H.-D. (2003). Redesigning literature: The cinematic poetics of American Sign Language poetry. *Sign Language Studies, 4*(1), 34–47.

Bellugi, U. (1980). Clues from the similarities between signed and spoken languages. In U. Bellugi & M. Studdert-Kennedy (Eds.), *Signed and spoken language: Biological constraints on linguistic form* (pp. 115–140). Weinheim, Germany: Verlag Chemie.

Bess, F., Dodd-Murphy, J., & Parker, R. (1998). Children with minimal sensorineural hearing loss: Prevalence, educational performance, and functional status. *Ear and Hearing, 19*(5), 339–354.

Blamey, P. (2003). Development of spoken language by deaf children. In M. Marschark & P. Spencer (Eds.), *Oxford handbook of deaf studies, language, and education* (pp. 232–246). New York: Oxford University Press.

Blamey, P., Sarant, J., Paatsch, L., Barry, J., Bow, C., Wales, R., et al. (2001). Relationships among speech perception, production, language, hearing loss, and age in children with impaired hearing. *Journal of Speech, Language, and Hearing Research, 44*(2), 264–285.

Bourdieu, P. (1977). The economics of linguistic exchanges. *Social Science Information, 16*(6), 645–668.

Canadian Institute of Child Health (2001). *A preliminary evaluation of the Parent-Child Mother Goose Program as a family literacy program*. Ottawa, Ontario, Canada: Author.

Chamberlain, C., & Mayberry, R. (2000). Theorizing about the relation between American Sign Language and reading. In C. Chamberlain, J. Morford, & R. Mayberry (Eds.), *Language acquisition by eye* (pp. 221–259). Mahwah, NJ: Lawrence Erlbaum Associates.

Cohen, L., Manion, L., & Morrison, K. (2000). *Research methods in education* (5th ed.). London: Routledge Falmer.

Comeau, L., Genesee, F., & Lapaquette, L. (2003). The modeling hypothesis and child bilingual codemixing. *International Journal of Bilingualism, 7*, 113–126.

Cripps, J. (2000). *Quiet journey: Understanding the rights of Deaf children*. Owen Sound, Ontario, Canada: Ginger Press.

Cummins, J. (1981). The role of primary language development in promoting educational success for language minority students. In

California State Department of Education (Ed.), *Schooling and language minority students: A theoretical framework* (pp. 3–49). Los Angeles: Evaluation, Dissemination and Assessment Center, California State University.

Cummins, J. (1997). Minority status and schooling in Canada. *Anthropology & Education Quarterly, 28*(3), 411–430.

Cummins, J. (2001). *Negotiating identities: Education for empowerment in a diverse society* (2nd ed.). Covina, CA: California Association for Bilingual Education.

Cummins, J. (2005, September). *Teaching for cross-language transfer in dual language education: Possibilities and pitfalls.* Paper presented at the TESOL Symposium on Dual Language Education: Teaching and Learning Two Languages in the EFL Setting. Bogazici University, Istanbul, Turkey.

Davies, S. (1991). The transition toward bilingual education of Deaf children in Sweden and Denmark: Perspectives on language. *Sign Language Studies, 71*, 169–195.

Delpit, L. (1988). The silenced dialogue: Power and pedagogy in educating other people's children. *Harvard Educational Review, 58*(3), 280–298.

Durieux-Smith, A., & Whittingham, J. (2000). The rationale for neonatal hearing screening. *Journal of Speech-Language Pathology and Audiology, 24*, 59–67.

Egan, K. (1987). Literacy and the oral foundations of education. *Harvard Educational Review, 57*(4), 445–472.

Ellsworth, E. (1989). Why doesn't this feel empowering? Working through the repressive myths of critical pedagogy. *Harvard Educational Review, 59*(3), 297–324.

Emery, S. (2003). Working through the pain of change. In Deaf Ex-Mainstreamers Group (Ed.), *Between a rock and a hard place* (pp. 17–21). Wakefield, West Yorkshire, England: Deaf Ex-Mainstreamers Group.

Emery, S. D., Middleton, A., & Turner, G. H. (2010). Whose deaf genes are they anyway? The deaf community's challenge to legislation on embryo selection. *Sign Language Studies, 10*(2), 155–169.

Emmorey, K. (2002). *Language, cognition and the brain: Insights from sign language research.* Mahwah, NJ: Lawrence Erlbaum Associates.

Eriks-Brophy, A. (2004). Outcomes of auditory-verbal therapy: A review of the evidence and a call for action. *Volta Review, 104*(1), 21–35.

Erting, L., & Pfau, J. (1997). *Becoming bilingual: Facilitating English literacy development using ASL in preschool.* Washington, DC: Gallaudet University Laurent Clerc National Deaf Education Center.

Fjord, L. (1999). "Voices offstage": How vision has become a symbol to resist in an audiology lab in the U.S. *Visual Anthropology Review, 15*(2), 121–138.

Foucault, M. (1972). *The archaeology of knowledge.* New York: Harper Colophon.

Freire, P. (2000). *Pedagogy of the oppressed* (30th anniversary ed.). New York: Continuum.

Gee, J. P. (2008). *Social linguistics and literacies: Ideology in Discourses* (3rd ed.). London: Routledge.

Genesee, F., Nicoladis, E., & Paradis, J. (1995). Language differentiation in early bilingual development. *Journal of Child Language, 22,* 611–631.

Goldin-Meadow, S., & Mayberry, R. (2001). How do profoundly deaf children learn to read? *Learning Disabilities Research and Practice, 16*(4), 222–229.

Goodwyn, S., Acredolo, L., & Brown, C. (2000). Impact of symbolic gesturing on early language development. *Journal of Nonverbal Behavior, 24*(2), 81–103.

Haptonstall-Nykaza, T., & Schick, B. (2007). The transition from fingerspelling to English print: Facilitating English decoding. *Journal of Deaf Studies and Deaf Education, 12*(2), 172–183.

Haualand, H., & Hansen, I. (2007). A study of Norwegian deaf and hard of hearing children: Equality in communication inside and outside family life. In L. Komesaroff (Ed.), *Surgical consent: Bioethics and cochlear implantation* (pp. 151–164). Washington, DC: Gallaudet University Press.

Hearing Loss Association of America (2009). *Government assistance: State mandates for hearing aid insurance.* Retrieved from http://www .hearingloss.org/advocacy/govtassistance.asp

Heath, S. (1983). *Ways with words: Language, life, and work in communities and classrooms.* Cambridge, England: Cambridge University Press.

Hemingway, J. (Writer/Director). (2007). *Classic Ontario ASL: Name signs* [Motion picture]. Available from the Canadian Cultural Society of the Deaf, www.deafculturecentre.ca

Hoffmeister, R. (2000). A piece of the puzzle: ASL and reading comprehension in deaf children. In C. Chamberlain, J. Morford, & R. Mayberry (Eds.), *Language acquisition by eye* (pp. 143–163). Mahwah, NJ: Lawrence Erlbaum Associates.

Hyde, M. (2002). Ontario's infant hearing and communication development program. *Public Health and Epidemiology Report Ontario, 13*(9), 176–182.

Hyde, M., Friedberg, J., Price, D., & Weber, S. (2004). Ontario Infant Hearing Program: Program overview, implications for physicians. *Ontario Medical Review, 71*(1), 1–6.

Israelite, N., & Ewoldt, C. (1992). *Bilingual/bicultural education for deaf and hard-of-hearing students: A review of the literature on the effects of native sign language on majority language acquisition.* Toronto, Ontario, Canada: Queen's Printer for Ontario.

Jones, J. (2003). J's feelings. In Deaf Ex-Mainstreamers Group (Ed.), *Between a rock and a hard place.* Wakefield, West Yorkshire, England: Deaf Ex-Mainstreamers Group.

Knecht, H., Nelson, P., Whitelaw, G., & Feth, L. (2002). Background noise levels and reverberation times in unoccupied classrooms: Predictions and measurements. *American Journal of Audiology, 11*, 65–71.

Komesaroff, L. (2007). Introduction. In L. Komesaroff (Ed.), *Surgical consent: Bioethics and cochlear implantation.* Washington, DC: Gallaudet University Press.

Komesaroff, L. (2008). *Disabling pedagogy: Power, politics, and deaf education.* Washington, DC: Gallaudet University Press.

Kourbetis, V. (1982). *Education of the deaf in Greece.* First International Conference on Education of the Deaf, Athens, Greece.

Ladd, P. (2003). *Understanding deaf culture: In search of Deafhood.* Clevedon, England: Multilingual Matters.

Ladd, P. (2007). Cochlear implantation, colonialism, and Deaf rights. In L. Komesaroff (Ed.), *Surgical consent: Bioethics and cochlear implantation* (pp. 1–29). Washington, DC: Gallaudet University Press.

Lane, H. (1992). *The mask of benevolence: Disabling the deaf community.* New York: Vintage.

Lane, H., Hoffmeister, R., & Bahan, B. (1996). *A journey into the Deaf-World.* San Diego, CA: DawnSign Press.

Lather, P. (1986). Issues of validity in openly ideological research. *Interchange, 17*(4), 63–84.

Lenneberg, E. (1967) *Biological foundations of language.* New York: Wiley.

Lo Bianco, J. (2001). From policy to anti-policy: How fear of language rights took policy-making out of community hands. In J. Lo Bianco

& R. Wickert (Eds.), *Australian policy activism in language and literacy* (pp. 13–44). Canberra: Language Australia.

Lucas, C., Valli, C., Mulrooney, K., & Villanueva, M. (2011). *Linguistics of American Sign Language* (5th ed.). Washington, DC: Gallaudet University Press.

Macedo, D. (1993). Literacy for stupidification: The pedagogy of big lies. *Harvard Educational Review, 63*(2), 183–206.

Mahshie, S. (1995). *Educating deaf children bilingually: With insights and applications from Sweden and Denmark*. Washington, DC: Pre-College Programs, Gallaudet University.

Mayberry, R. (1993). First-language acquisition after childhood differs from second- language acquisition: The case of American Sign Language. *Journal of Speech and Hearing Research, 36*, 1258–1270.

Mayberry, R. (1994). The importance of childhood to language acquisition: Evidence from American Sign Language. In J. Goodman & H. Nusbaum (Eds.), *The development of speech perception: The transition from speech sounds to spoken words* (pp. 57–90). Cambridge, MA: MIT Press.

Mayberry, R., & Eichen, E. (1991). The long-lasting advantage of learning sign language in childhood: Another look at the critical period for language acquisition. *Journal of Memory and Language, 30*, 486–512.

Mayer, C., & Wells, G. (1996). Can the linguistic interdependence theory support a bilingual-bicultural model of literacy education for deaf students? *Journal of Deaf Studies and Deaf Education, 1*(2), 93–107.

McKee, R. (2008). The construction of deaf children as marginal bilinguals in the mainstream. *International Journal of Bilingual Education and Bilingualism, 11*(5), 519–540.

McQuarrie, L., & Parrila, R. (2009). Phonological representations in deaf children: Rethinking the "Functional Equivalence" hypothesis. *Journal of Deaf Studies and Deaf Education, 14*(2), 137–154.

Meadow, K. (1977). Name signs as identity symbols in the deaf community. *Sign Language Studies, 16*, 237–246.

Meadow-Orlans, K. (2004). Participant characteristics and research procedures. In K. Meadow-Orlans, P. Spencer, & L. Koester (Eds.), *The world of deaf infants: A longitudinal study* (pp. 24–39). New York: Oxford University Press.

Meadow-Orlans, K., Mertens, D., & Sass-Lehrer, M. (2003). *Parents and their deaf children: The early years*. Washington, DC: Gallaudet University Press.

Meadow-Orlans, K., Spencer, P., Koester, L., & Steinberg, A. (2004). Implications for intervention with infants and families. In K. Meadow-Orlans, P. Spencer, & L. Koester (Eds.), *The world of deaf infants: A longitudinal study* (pp. 218–228). New York: Oxford University Press.

Mindess, A. (1990). What name signs can tell us about Deaf culture. *Sign Language Studies, 66*, 1–21.

Ministry of Children & Youth Services (2010). *Ontario Early Years Centres frequently asked questions.* Retrieved from http://www.children.gov.on.ca/htdocs/English/topics/earlychildhood/oeyc/questio ns/index.aspx#what

Morford, J., & Mayberry, R. (2000). A reexamination of "early exposure" and its implications for language acquisition by eye. In C. Chamberlain, J. Morford, & R. Mayberry (Eds.), *Language acquisition by eye* (pp. 111–127). Mahwah, NJ: Lawrence Erlbaum Associates.

Neville, H. (1988). Cerebral organization for spatial attention. In J. Stiles-Davis, M. Kritchevsky, & U. Bellugi (Eds.), *Spatial cognition: Brain bases and development* (pp. 327–341). Hillsdale, NJ: Hove.

Neville, H. (1991). Neurobiology of cognitive and language processing: Effects of early experience. In K. Gibson & A. Petersen (Eds.), *Brain maturation and behavioural development* (pp. 355–380). Hawthorn, NY: Aldine Gruyter Press.

Neville, H., & Bellugi, U. (1978). Patterns of cerebral specialization in congenitally deaf adults: A preliminary report. In P. Siple (Ed.), *Understanding language through sign language research* (pp. 239–257). New York: Academic Press.

New London Group (1996). A pedagogy of multiliteracies: Designing social futures. *Harvard Educational Review, 66*, 60–92.

Newport, E. (1990). Maturational constraints on language learning. *Cognitive Science, 14*, 11–28.

Newport, E. (1991). Contrasting conceptions of the critical period for language. In S. Carey & R. Gelman (Eds.), *The epigenesis of mind: Essays on biology and cognition* (pp. 111–130). Hillsdale, NJ: Lawrence Erlbaum Associates.

Newport, E., & Meier, R. (1985). The acquisition of American Sign Language. In D. Slobin (Ed.), *The crosslinguistic study of language acquisition: Vol. 1* (pp. 881–938). Hillsdale, NJ: Lawrence Erlbaum Associates.

Norton Peirce, B. (1995). Social identity, investment, and language learning. *TESOL Quarterly, 29*(1), 9–31.

Ogbu, J. (1992). Understanding cultural diversity and learning. *Educational Researcher, 21*(8), 5–14.

Ogbu, J. (1993). Variability in minority school performance: A problem in search of an explanation. In E. Jacob & C. Jordan (Eds.), *Minority education: Anthropological perspectives* (pp. 83–111). Norwood, NJ: Ablex.

Padden, C. (1992). Foreword. In Supalla, S., *The book of name signs: Naming in American Sign Language* (pp. ix–x). San Diego, CA: DawnSign Press.

Padden, C., & Humphries, T. (2005). *Inside deaf culture*. Cambridge, MA: Harvard University Press.

Padden, C., & Ramsey, C. (1998). Reading ability in signing deaf children. *Topics in Language Disorders, 18*(4), 30–47.

Padden, C., & Ramsey, C. (2000). American Sign Language and reading ability in deaf children. In C. Chamberlain, J. Morford, & R. Mayberry (Eds.), *Language acquisition by eye* (pp. 165–189). Mahwah, NJ: Lawrence Erlbaum Associates.

The Parent-Child Mother Goose Program (n.d.). *About Us*. Retrieved from http://www.nald.ca/mothergooseprogram/About.htm

Peterson, P. (2007). Freedom of speech for deaf people. In L. Komesaroff (Ed.), *Surgical consent: Bioethics and cochlear implantation* (pp. 165–173). Washington, DC: Gallaudet University Press.

Petitto, L. (1994). Are signed languages "real" languages? Evidence from American Sign Language and Langue des signes québécoise. *Signpost, 7*(3), 1–10.

Petitto, L. (2000). On the biological foundations of human language. In K. Emmorey & H. Lane (Eds.), *The signs of language revisited: An anthology in honour of Ursula Bellugi and Edward Klima* (pp. 449–473). Mahwah, NJ: Lawrence Erlbaum Associates.

Petitto, L., & Marentette, P. (1991). Babbling in the manual mode: Evidence for the ontogeny of language. *Science, 251*, 1483–1496.

Picard, M., & Bradley, J. (2001). Revisiting speech interference in classrooms. *Audiology, 40*, 221–244.

Preisler, G. (1999). The development of communication and language in deaf and severely hard of hearing children: Implications for the future. *International Journal of Pediatric Otorhinolaryngology, 49*, S39–S43.

Preisler, G., & Ahlström, M. (1997). Sign language for hard of hearing children: A hindrance or a benefit for their development? *European Journal of Psychology of Education, 12*(4), 465–477.

Preisler, G., Tvingstedt, A., & Ahlström, M. (2002). A psychosocial follow-up study of deaf preschool children using cochlear implants. *Child: Care, Health and Development, 28*(5), 403–418.

Preisler, G., Tvingstedt, A., & Ahlström, M. (2005). Interviews with deaf children about their experiences using cochlear implants. *American Annals of the Deaf, 150*(3), 260–267.

Provincial Court of Saskatchewan. (2005, August 19). The Child and Family Services Act of Saskatchewan and Ryley Allen Farnham, the Honourable Justice Orr, P.C.J.

Roberts, L. (1998). *The outreach ASL program* (2nd ed.). Belleville, Ontario, Canada: Sir James Whitney School for the Deaf Resource Services.

Sass-Lehrer, M., & Bodner-Johnson, B. (2003). Early intervention: Current approaches to family-centered programming. In M. Marschark & P. Spencer (Eds.), *Oxford handbook of deaf studies, language and education* (pp. 65–81). New York: Oxford University Press.

Schick, B. (2003). The development of American Sign Language and manually coded English systems. In M. Marschark & P. Spencer (Eds.), *Oxford handbook of deaf studies, language and education* (pp. 219–231). New York: Oxford University Press.

Schick, B., Marschark, M., & Spencer, P. (2006). Preface. In B. Schick, M. Marschark, & P. Spencer (Eds.), *Advances in the sign language development of deaf children* (pp.v–xii). New York: Oxford University Press.

Shield, B., & Dockrell, J. (2004). External and internal noise surveys of London primary schools. *Journal of the Acoustical Society of America, 115,* 730–738.

Singleton, J., Supalla, S., Litchfield, S., & Schley, S. (1998). From sign to word: Considering modality constraints in ASL/English bilingual education. *Topics in Language Disorders 18*(4), 16–30.

Small, A., & Cripps, J. (2004). Questions parents ask. In K. Snoddon, A. Small, & J. Cripps (Eds.), *A parent guidebook: ASL and early literacy* (pp. 45–63). Mississauga, Ontario, Canada: Ontario Cultural Society of the Deaf.

Small, A., & Mason, D. (2008). ASL bilingual bicultural education. In J. Cummins & N. Hornberger (Eds.), *Encyclopedia of language and education: Volume 5. Bilingual education* (2nd ed., pp. 133–149). New York: Springer.

Snoddon, K. (2008). American Sign Language and early intervention. *Canadian Modern Language Review, 64*(4), 581–604.

Snoddon, K. (2010). Technology as a learning tool for ASL literacy. *Sign Language Studies, 10*.

Snow, C., Burns, M., & Griffin, P. (1998). *Preventing reading difficulties in young children*. Washington, DC: National Academy Press.

Spencer, P. (2002). Closing presentation: Considerations for the future: Putting it all together. *Cochlear Implants and Sign Language: Putting it All Together* (Identifying Effective Practices for Educational Settings conference proceedings, pp. 23–29). Washington, DC: Laurent Clerc National Deaf Education Center.

Spencer, P. (2004). Language at 12 and 18 months: Characteristics and accessibility of linguistic models. In K. Meadow-Orlans, P. Spencer, & L. Koester (Eds.), *The world of deaf infants: A longitudinal study* (pp. 147–167). New York: Oxford University Press.

Spencer, P., & Marschark, M. (2003). Cochlear implants: issues and implications. In M. Marschark & P. Spencer (Eds.), *Oxford handbook of deaf studies, language, and education* (pp. 434–448). New York: Oxford University Press.

Stredler-Brown, A., & Arehart, K. (2000). Universal newborn hearing screening: Impact on early intervention services. *Volta Review, 100*(5), 85–117.

Strong, M., & Prinz, P. (1997). A study of the relationship between American Sign Language and English literacy. *Journal of Deaf Studies and Deaf Education, 2*(1), 37–46.

Strong, M., & Prinz, P. (2000). Is American Sign Language skill related to English literacy? In C. Chamberlain, J. Morford, & R. Mayberry (Eds.), *Language acquisition by eye* (pp. 131–141). Mahwah, NJ: Lawrence Erlbaum Associates.

Supalla, S. (1990). The arbitrary name sign system in American Sign Language. *Sign Language Studies, 67*, 99–126.

Supalla, S. (1992). *The book of name signs: Naming in American Sign Language*. San Diego, CA: DawnSign Press.

Swedish National Board of Health & Welfare. (2000). *Vårdprogram för barn med cochlea implantat* [Directions for habilitation of children with cochlear implants]. Report no. 2000:06.

Valli, C. (1990). The nature of the line in ASL poetry. In W. Edmonson & F. Karlsson (Eds.), *Papers from the 1987 Fourth International Symposium on Sign Language Research*. Hamburg, Germany: Signum.

Valli, C. (Writer). (1995). *ASL poetry: The selected works of Clayton Valli* [Motion picture]. San Diego, CA: DawnSign Press.

Valli, C., & Lucas, C. (1995). *Linguistics of American Sign Language: An introduction* (2nd ed.). Washington, DC: Gallaudet University Press.

Volterra, V., & Iverson, J. (1995). When do modality factors affect the course of language acquisition? In K. Emmorey & J. Reilly (Eds.), *Language, gesture and space* (pp. 371–390). Hillsdale, NJ: Lawrence Erlbaum Associates.

Volterra, V., Iverson, J., & Castrataro, M. (2006). The development of gesture in hearing and deaf children. In B. Schick, M. Marschark, & P. Spencer (Eds.), *Advances in the sign language development of deaf children* (pp. 46–70). New York: Oxford University Press.

Watkins, S., Pittman, P., & Walden, B. (1998). The deaf mentor experimental project for young children who are deaf and their families. *American Annals of the Deaf, 143*(1), 29–35.

Weisel, A. (1988). Parental hearing status, reading comprehension skills and social-emotional adjustment. *American Annals of the Deaf, 133*, 356–359.

Yoshinaga-Itano, C. (2006). Early identification, communication modality, and the development of speech and spoken language skills: Patterns and considerations. In P. Spencer & M. Marschark (Eds.), *Advances in the spoken language development of deaf and hard-of-hearing children* (pp. 298–327). New York: Oxford University Press.

Yoshinaga-Itano, C., & Sedey, A. (2000). Early speech development in children who are deaf or hard of hearing: Interrelationships with language and hearing. *Volta Review, 100*(5), 181–211.

Yoshinaga-Itano, C., Sedey, A., Coulter, D., & Mehl, A. (1998). The language of early- and later-identified children with hearing loss. *Pediatrics, 102*, 1161–1171.

Zweibel, A. (1987). More on the effects of early manual communication on the cognitive development of deaf children. *American Annals of the Deaf, 132*, 16–20.

Author's Note

Several ASL rhymes described in this book (and other ASL rhymes) can be viewed on two DVDs that are available through the Canadian Cultural Society of the Deaf (CCSD) at www.deafculturecentre.ca:

- *The ASL Parent-Child Mother Goose Program: American Sign Language rhymes, rhythms and stories for parents and their children* (Ontario Cultural Society of the Deaf, 2004).
- *ASL rhymes, rhythms, & stories for you and your child* (Ontario Cultural Society of the Deaf, 2008).

CCSD also provides training for ASL-fluent people who are interested in learning how to become certified ASL Parent-Child Mother Goose Program leaders.

Index